NML EXP

D1323243

Natsuko Imamura was born in Hiroshima, Japan, in 1980. Her fiction has won various prestigious Japanese literary prizes, including the Noma Literary New Face Prize, the Mishima Yukio Prize, and the Akutagawa Prize. She lives in Osaka with her husband and daughter.

Further praise for *The Woman in the Purple Skirt*:

'Short and spare, Imamura's clever and engrossing English language debut deals with loneliness and voyeurism in ways that are alternately chilling, poignant and humorous.' *Herald*

'Sparkles with a style that is clean, understated and funny . . . In a world that was already grappling with a loneliness epidemic before Covid-19, Imamura's book is a timely read.' *Straits Times*

'Horrifying, humorous, whimsical, and disturbing . . . It will remain with you.' *Tokyo Shimbun*

'A novel unlike anything that's come before it . . . This strange and unsettling story about control and paranoia will likely take 2021 by storm.' *Metropolis*

'An unsettling story of obsession that you never see coming.' *Chicago Tribune*

'A defiant and hysterical ode to the power of the woman alone.' *CrimeReads*

'Deliciously creepy . . . Imamura's pacing is as deft and quick as the best thrillers, but her prose is also understated and quietly subtle . . . A subtly ominous story about voyeurism and the danger of losing yourself in someone else . . . A resounding success.' *Kirkus*

'Imamura's spare, intense prose calls to mind Sayaka Murata's *Convenience Store Woman* with an extra edge of danger.' *Booklist*

'Graceful . . . The narrator's intense one-way nonsexual desire creates an off-balance frisson of strangeness . . . infused with the power of fascination . . . [For] psychological thriller fans who appreciate subtlety.' *Publishers Weekly*

'I adore the way this book possesses a quality to get under your skin . . . You can't look away.' *Book Riot*

'Imamura's latest is like Anita Brookner's *Look at Me*, reimagined by a surrealist.' *Vulture*

'Bold and compelling . . . Well written and engaging . . . Imamura's strong prose creates an atmosphere of menace that is tense and creepy . . . An eerie window into Japan's darker side.' *The Lady*

'Reading this novel, you can really hear Natsuko Imamura's unique voice, which comes across quite unsparingly and beautifully.' Hiromi Kawakami

'A superb story . . . I was mesmerized by this narrator. Unlikeable men who hold our sympathy are frequently found in fiction, but I don't think I've ever encountered a woman as unappealing as this one who still managed to keep me completely beguiled.' Shuichi Yoshida

'*The Woman in the Purple Skirt* is like a love story overheard on a park bench. It's a thriller about commutes, work schedules, and unemployment . . . What profound and giddy prose; I could not put this book down. Imamura is a glorious architect of perspective, surprising and breaking this reader's heart at every turn.' Hilary Leichter

'I tore through this novel. Grippingly and intimately told, with prose as tight as a wire, *The Woman in the Purple Skirt* is a quick and powerful jab to the heart.' Jami Attenberg

'Delightful, droll, and menacing, this novel about a seemingly harmless obsession could be the love child of Eugène Ionesco and Patricia Highsmith.' Kelly Link

'The Woman in the Purple Skirt expertly balances between the mundane and the extraordinary, never swerving too far towards one side. Written with clinical prose and a wry sense of humor, Imamura shows us that the most powerful portrayal of loneliness is not through the self, but the projection of the self onto another.' An Yu

THE WOMAN IN THE PURPLE SKIRT

NATSUKO IMAMURA

Translated from the Japanese by
LUCY NORTH

faber

First published in the UK in 2021
by Faber & Faber Limited
Bloomsbury House
74–77 Great Russell Street
London WC1B 3DA

First published in the USA in 2021
by Penguin Books, an imprint of
Penguin Random House LLC

This paperback edition first published in 2022

Originally published in Japanese as『むらさきのスカートの女』
(*Murasaki no sukato no onna*) by Asahi Shimbun Publications, Inc.

Designed by Sabrina Bowers
Printed and bound by CPI Group (UK) Ltd, Croydon, CR0 4YY

All rights reserved
Copyright © 2019 by Natsuko Imamura
Translation copyright © 2021 by Lucy North

The right of Natsuko Imamura to be identified as author of this work
has been asserted in accordance with Section 77 of the Copyright,
Designs and Patents Act 1988

*This is a work of fiction. All of the characters, organizations, and events
portrayed in this novel are either products of the author's imagination or
are used fictitiously.*

*This book is sold subject to the condition that it shall not, by way of trade
or otherwise, be lent, resold, hired out or otherwise circulated without the
publisher's prior consent in any form of binding or cover other than that
in which it is published and without a similar condition including this
condition being imposed on the subsequent purchaser*

A CIP record for this book
is available from the British Library

ISBN 978-0-571-36468-8

MIX
Paper from
responsible sources
FSC® C171272

2 4 6 8 10 9 7 5 3 1

THE WOMAN IN THE

PURPLE SKIRT

THERE'S A PERSON LIVING NOT TOO FAR FROM me known as the Woman in the Purple Skirt. She only ever wears a purple-colored skirt—which is why she has this name.

At first I thought the Woman in the Purple Skirt must be a young girl. This is probably because she is small and delicate looking, and because she has long hair that hangs down loosely over her shoulders. From a distance, you'd be forgiven for thinking she was about thirteen. But look carefully, from up close, and you see she's not young—far from it. She has age spots on her cheeks, and that shoulder-length black hair is not glossy—it's quite dry and stiff. About once a week, the Woman in the Purple Skirt goes to a bakery in the local shopping district and buys herself a little custard-filled cream bun. I always pretend to be taking my time deciding which pastries to buy, but in reality I'm getting a good look at her. And as I watch, I think to myself: She reminds me of somebody. But who?

There's even a bench, a special bench in the local park, that's known as the Woman in the Purple Skirt's Exclusively Reserved Seat. It's one of three benches on the park's south side—the farthest from the entrance.

On certain days, I've seen the Woman in the Purple Skirt purchase her cream bun from the bakery, walk through the shopping district, and head straight for the park. The time is just past three in the afternoon. The evergreen oaks that border the south side of the park provide shade for the Exclusively Reserved Seat. The Woman in the Purple Skirt sits down in the middle of the bench and proceeds to eat her cream bun, holding one hand cupped underneath it, in case any of the custard filling spills onto her lap. After gazing for a second or two at the top of the bun, which is decorated with sliced almonds, she pops that too into her mouth, and proceeds to chew her last mouthful particularly slowly and lingeringly.

As I watch her, I think to myself:

I know: the Woman in the Purple Skirt bears a resemblance to my sister! Of course, I'm aware that she is not actually my sister. Their faces are totally different.

But my sister was also one of those people who take their time with that last mouthful. Normally mild mannered, and happy to let me, the younger of the two of us, prevail in any of our sibling squabbles, my sister was a complete obsessive when it came to food. Her favorite was *purin*—the caramel custard cups available at every supermarket and convenience store. After eating it, she would often stare for ten, even twenty minutes at the caramel sauce, just dipping the little plastic spoon into it. I remember once, unable to bear it, swiping the cup out of her hands. "Give it to me, if you're not going to eat it!" The fight that ensued—stuff pulled to the floor, furniture tipped over . . . I still have scars on my upper arms from her scratches, and I'm sure she still has the teeth marks I left on her thumb. It's been twenty years since my parents divorced and the family broke apart. I wonder where my sister is now, and what she's doing. Here I am thinking she still loves *purin*, but who knows, things change, and she too has probably changed.

If the Woman in the Purple Skirt bears a resemblance to my sister, then maybe that means she is like me . . . ? No? But it's not as if we have nothing in common. For now, let's just say she's the Woman in the Purple Skirt, and I'm the Woman in the Yellow Cardigan.

Unfortunately, no one knows or cares about the Woman in the Yellow Cardigan. That's the difference between her and the Woman in the Purple Skirt.

When the Woman in the Yellow Cardigan goes out walking in the shopping district, nobody pays the slightest bit of attention. But when the Woman in the Purple Skirt goes out, it's impossible not to pay attention. Nobody could ignore her.

Say if she were to appear at the other end of the arcade. Everybody would immediately react—in one of four broad ways. Some people would pretend they hadn't seen her, and carry on as before. Others would quickly move aside, to give her room to pass. Some would pump their fists, and look happy and hopeful. Others would do the opposite, and look fearful and downcast. (It's one of the rules that two sightings in a single day means good luck, while three means bad luck.)

The most incredible thing about the Woman in the Purple Skirt is that whatever reaction she gets from people around her, it makes absolutely no difference—she just continues on her way. Maintaining that same steady pace, lightly, quickly, smoothly moving through the crowd. Strangely enough, even on weekends, at peak times when the streets are jam-packed with shoppers, she never walks into anyone, or bumps into anything—she just walks swiftly on, unimpeded. I would say that to be able to do that, either she has to be in possession of superb speed, agility, and fitness—or she has an extra eye fixed to her forehead, a third eye skillfully concealed under her bangs, rotating 360 degrees, giving her a good view of whatever's coming her way. Whichever it is, it's a trick well beyond the capability of the Woman in the Yellow Cardigan.

She's so skillful at avoiding any sort of collision that I can understand why you might get a rather eccentric person coming along who feels provoked— and gets the urge to purposely barge into her. Actually, there was one time when I myself succumbed to just such an urge. But of course, I was no more successful than anyone else. When was it? I think sometime in early spring. I pretended to be walking along innocently, minding my own business, and then, when the Woman in the Purple Skirt was just a few feet ahead of me, I suddenly upped my speed and walked very fast toward her.

A pretty stupid thing to do, as I soon found out. When I was within inches of bumping into her, the Woman in the Purple Skirt simply tilted her body slightly to one side, and I went smack into the meat display cabinet in front of the butcher shop— fortunately escaping any serious physical injury, but still ending up with a huge repair bill from the butcher.

That happened more than six months ago now. I've only just paid off the bill. And it wasn't easy. I had to resort to sneaking my way into the bazaars held at a local primary school, having picked up anything that might possibly sell, to make whatever extra pennies I could. The first few times, I'd be thinking: Now look where your stupidity has landed you. Do not try anything like that ever again. It's common knowledge that nobody who has attempted to collide with the Woman in the Purple Skirt has ever succeeded—don't you know that? If not because of that third eye on her forehead, then because of how uncannily quick and fit she is. Even if privately you can't help feeling that "fit" isn't quite the right word to describe her. . . . Actually, it occurs to me that the way she has of swerving smoothly through the crowds, avoiding all oncoming people, is very much like the way an ice-skater glides around on the ice. She is like that girl who won a bronze medal a couple of years ago at the Winter Olympics— the one in a blue skating dress who spoke in that strange way, like a little old lady, and who retired from skating to go into television and was selected last year to be a presenter on children's TV; she was ranked number one in the children's TV popularity rankings—yes, that girl. Admittedly, the Woman in the Purple Skirt is quite a bit older than she is, but (in my neighborhood, at least) she is every bit as famous.

It's true. The Woman in the Purple Skirt is a celebrity. In the eyes of everyone—children and adults. From time to time, TV camera crews come by this area to conduct interviews with people on the street. But rather than thrusting a microphone in the faces of housewives and interrogating them about their dinner plans or their opinions on the rising price of vegetables, they should occasionally direct questions at elderly people and children. *Have you ever heard of the Woman in the Purple Skirt?* I'm sure nearly everyone would say: Yes, of course!

There's even a new game that the children have taken to playing. Whoever loses at rock-paper-scissors now has to go up to the Woman in the Purple Skirt and give her a light tap. It's a minor variation on the usual game, but they all get very excited about it. It takes place in the park. Any child who loses a round has to tiptoe up to the Woman in the Purple Skirt as she sits on her Exclusively Reserved Seat and give her a little tap on the shoulder. That's all it is. Once the child has tapped her, he or she runs away laughing. They do this over and over again.

Originally, the addition involved not touching the Woman in the Purple Skirt but just approaching her and addressing her. The loser had to go over to her as she sat there and just say a few words. "Hello!" "Beautiful day!" Anything. That in itself was the source of huge amusement. Each child would skip up to her, say a word or two, and dash away, cackling with laughter.

It's only recently that the new twist was devised. The reason seems to have been simply that both sides had grown bored with the previous version. All they could think of to say to her was, "Are you well?" "Nice weather!" Or at best something like "Haa waa yuu?" in English—which of course didn't get a peep out of her. The Woman in the Purple Skirt sat absolutely still, her eyes lowered, but as time passed, she would yawn or pick at her nails. As I watched her languidly plucking the pilling off her sweater, it almost seemed like she was trying to challenge the children to think of something new.

This new spin on the game, which the children came up with by forming a circle, putting their foreheads together, and thinking hard about how to break out of the old routine, is already showing signs of becoming the go-to version, and so far nobody's said they're tired of it. "Rock! Paper! Scissors!" they all yell. Up leaps the winner with a shout of triumph, while the loser wails with a look of misery. Meanwhile, there she sits, absolutely still, on her Exclusively Reserved Seat, her eyes lowered, her hands in her lap. It's possible she's not comfortable with this new rule. I wonder what's going through her mind when she gets that little tap on her shoulder.

I KNOW I SAID THE WOMAN IN THE PURPLE Skirt reminded me of my sister. But actually, I think I was wrong. And she's not like that figure skater turned celebrity either. The person she most reminds me of is Mei-chan, a friend I had in elementary school. A girl who used to wear her hair in long braids secured with red elastic bands. Mei-chan's father came from China. Just a day or so before our elementary school graduation ceremony, Mei-chan's entire family had to go back to Shanghai, the father's home city. When the Woman in the Purple Skirt sits motionless on her bench, she reminds me of Mei-chan during swimming class. Not even looking at the rest of us as we swam around in the pool, but just sitting, hunched over, picking at her nails. Mei-chan? No . . . Could it be you? We lost touch after you returned to China, but . . . have you really come back all this way . . . to see me . . . ?

Come on—don't kid yourself. Mei-chan was a friend, but we were never actually close. We probably played together one or two times—at most. But Mei-chan was kind to me. I remember what she said about a picture I drew of a dog. "You've drawn that tail really well!" Child as I was, I felt so in awe of her. If anybody was good at drawing, it was Mei-chan. She always said she wanted to be a painter when she grew up. And that's exactly what she became. Fuan-Chun Mei, the Chinese painter who was brought up in Japan, and who just three years ago came back to Japan and had a solo exhibition. I saw a newspaper article about it. The woman standing in front of her paintings and smiling was definitely Mei-chan, even if she was no longer the little girl who wore her hair in braids. Ah yes, that's her, that's Mei-chan: the same big, bright eyes, the same beauty mark just below her nose.

The Woman in the Purple Skirt has small eyes that look sunken and narrow. She has age spots, yes, but not a single beauty mark.

If we're talking about eyes, the Woman in the

Purple Skirt reminds me of Arishima-san, my classmate in junior high school. Personality-wise, Arishima-san is probably one of a kind, but eye-wise, she is the spitting image. I was terrified of Arishima-san. She had her hair bleached blond like a real tough girl, she shoplifted, she extorted money from people, and she was violent. She carried a long knife like a Japanese sword everywhere she went. I think she was probably the most dangerous person I have ever met. Her parents, her teachers, even the police—no one knew what to do with her. I don't know why, but she once gave me a stick of plum-flavored chewing gum. I felt a poke in my back and heard someone say, "Want some gum?" That was the first time I looked at Arishima-san head-on. Those small, sunken, narrow eyes, those downwardly sloping eyebrows . . . For a second, I didn't know whom I was looking at.

I took the gum without saying anything. Why didn't I at least thank her? I assumed the gum was poisoned, and chucked it in a garbage can in front of a sake shop on my way home.

Why would it have been poisoned? I should have just started chewing it right there. The next day, I could have given her a piece of candy. Well, too late now. Arishima-san left school as soon as she could, after junior high, and immediately started hanging out with hoodlums. Rumor had it that she eventually got involved in pimping and drug dealing, and threw herself into gangster life. She's probably in jail now. On death row, maybe. Which means that the Woman in the Purple Skirt can't be her.

Oh, actually, there's another person the Woman in the Purple Skirt reminds me of. She's a regular commentator on afternoon TV shows. The manga artist who draws cutesy little cartoons about a ghost— and, just recently, illustrations for children's books. As she always says, it sounds so much better to be an "illustrator" than a "cartoonist," doesn't it? She's the one with the husband who is also a manga artist. What's his name? I can't remember.

Oh no, wait. The person the Woman in the Purple Skirt really reminds me of is the checkout girl in the supermarket near where I used to live. The woman who one day asked out of the blue whether I was okay. It was when things had hit rock bottom for me: I almost collapsed as I took my change from her. The next day, when I went again to the supermarket, she recognized me and called out a friendly greeting. I could never go back to that supermarket.

But recently, on a visit to the library in my old neighborhood, I dropped by the supermarket, for old times' sake, and took a peek inside. There she stood, in her usual place by the cash register. She looked well. I noticed yet another badge on the front of her uniform.

I think what I'm trying to say is that I've been wanting to become friends with the Woman in the Purple Skirt for a very long time.

I SHOULD ADD THAT I'VE ALREADY CHECKED out where the Woman in the Purple Skirt lives. I did that quite a long time ago. It's a ramshackle old apartment building not too far from the park. And, of course, not far from the shopping district either. Part of the roof is covered in blue tarp, and the handrail for the outside stairs connecting the floors is brown with rust. The Woman in the Purple Skirt glides up the stairs without even touching the railing. Her apartment is the one in the back corner on the second floor, farthest from the stairs. Apartment 201.

It's this apartment that the Woman in the Purple Skirt leaves when she goes to work. I have an idea, you know, that the people in the shopping district assume she doesn't work. And to be honest, that's what I too thought. A woman like that, I said to myself—I bet she's unemployed. That's what I assumed. But I was wrong. The Woman in the Purple Skirt is employed. How else would she be able to afford her cream bun or, for that matter, her rent?

But she doesn't work full time. Sometimes she is working, sometimes she is not. And her workplace seems to change over and over again. She's had a job at a screw-making factory, a toothbrush-making factory, an eye-drop-bottle-making factory . . . The jobs all seem to be for just a few days, or at most a few weeks. She'll be out of work for a really long time, then suddenly be employed for a whole month. I've written down her work record in my diary. Last year, in September, she was working. In October she didn't work. In November she worked for only the first half of the month. In December she was working, but for only the first half of the month. This year, her first job started on January 10. In February she worked. In March she worked. In April she didn't work. In May, apart from the annual Golden Week holiday, she was working. In June she worked. In July she worked. In August she worked for only the second half. In September she didn't work. In

October she worked on and off. And now, in November, it seems she is out of work.

When she does work, it is always at a job that involves getting up at the break of dawn and returning late in the evening. She comes straight home, obviously shattered, without stopping off anywhere to get something for dinner. If she does have a rare day off, she stays shut up inside her apartment.

Nowadays, I catch sight of her constantly, at all times of the day: sometimes in the park, sometimes in the shopping district. While it's difficult to keep tabs on her every minute of every hour, from the look of it I'd say the Woman in the Purple Skirt is in good health. And if she's in good health, you can be pretty certain she's out of work.

I want to become friends with the Woman in the Purple Skirt. But how?

That's all I can think about. But all that happens is that the days go by.

It would be weird to go up to her and say "Hi" out of the blue. I'm willing to bet that in her entire life the Woman in the Purple Skirt has probably never had anyone tell her they'd like to get to know her. I know I haven't. Does anyone ever have that said to them? It seems so forced. I just want to talk to her. It's not as if I'm making a pass at her.

But how do I go about it? I think the first thing to do would be to introduce myself formally to her— in a way that wouldn't feel too forced. Now, if we were students at the same school or coworkers in the same company, it might be possible.

SO HERE I AM IN THE PARK. I AM SITTING ON one of the three benches on the south side. The bench nearest the park entrance. In front of my face I'm holding yesterday's newspaper. I picked it out of the garbage can a few minutes ago.

The bench next to the bench next to mine is the Exclusively Reserved Seat. On the end of it is a magazine of job listings, the type available for free at any convenience store. Less than ten minutes ago, the Woman in the Purple Skirt was making her purchase in the bakery. If I know anything about her daily routine, she always drops by the park on days she goes to the bakery. And sure enough, just as I finish reading an entry in the advice column about a man in his thirties in the second year of a sexless marriage wondering if he should get a divorce, I hear the sound of her footsteps.

Hm. That was quick. I peer over the top of my

newspaper. It's a man dressed in an ordinary gray suit. So it wasn't her after all. On second thought, the sound of his footsteps was quite different. He trudges past me, letting the soles of his shoes drag along the ground, seemingly exhausted, and then plops himself down on the bench in the far corner.

Very likely a salaryman from some office in the city, out paying courtesy calls to potential clients. I notice he carries a black briefcase. Let me guess. Having traipsed into every remotely promising shop in the shopping district with not a single taker, he is now going to take a snooze in the park on the sly. There are five benches total in the park (three on the south side, two on the north). You can always tell the ones who are first-time visitors by the bench they choose. I felt sorry for him, seeing how exhausted he was. But tough luck. It was time to get him to move.

I approached him to explain the situation, but he just glanced up at me with a look of menace in his eyes. Even so, a reserved seat is a reserved seat. Rules are rules. I had no choice. I had to get him to give it up.

I repeated what I'd said several times, and finally the penny seemed to drop: he got up and moved to another bench, though with extreme reluctance. And just at this moment, out of the corner of my eye, I detected that someone else was approaching. This time it had to be her. I rushed back to my seat, and held my newspaper up in front of my face.

The Woman in the Purple Skirt carried a single paper bag from the bakery. After seating herself on her Exclusively Reserved Seat, which had just this minute been vacated, she opened up the bag and drew out her purchase. The usual cream bun. It's the kind of thing that is typically the subject of TV street interviews. "What did you buy today?" the interviewer asks, stopping shoppers who are carrying bags with the bakery logo and thrusting the microphone in their faces. The soft white loaf and the cream bun are the most common answers. And my answer too would be "A cream bun!" if anyone were to ask me. The distinctive features? Well, I'd say the custard filling, which has to have just the right degree of stiffness, and the delicately thin surrounding dough. Then there's the sprinkling of sliced almonds on top. That's what makes that satisfyingly crisp sound when you take a bite.

M-m-unch. Crunch-crunch-crunch. Some almond pieces fell onto the Woman in the Purple Skirt's skirt. Pitter-patter through the fingers of the hand she held underneath the bun as she ate. She didn't notice this. She always looked off in the distance as she ate her cream bun. Proof that she was concentrating. Her eyes and ears were closed to the world. That repeated crunching sound again. *Nom-nom. Crunch-crunch.* Yum. Delicious.

She finished eating the bun, then balled up the paper bag, and her eye fell on the jobs magazine on the end of the bench. In an unhurried way she picked it up and started flicking through it. After flicking quickly through it once, she went back to the beginning, then flicked through it again, this time more slowly. There was a special feature in this issue, "Best Workplaces for Team Players." It took up almost half the magazine. But that wasn't important, no, skip that. "Part-Time Work in the Hospitality Industry,"

"Part-Time Work in Clothing and Retail" . . . No, skip those too. The edges of the pages had different colors—blue, red, yellow, green—according to the type of work. The final pages, "Night Work," were pink edged. For some reason, she perused these pink pages at some length. No, not there. Look at the section preceding that, the one with the green edges. That small box advertisement to the right of "Parcel Sorters." I'd circled it with a fluorescent marker. It should've been obvious.

Had she seen it—had she got the hint? The Woman in the Purple Skirt closed the magazine, rolled it up, got to her feet, and headed toward the garbage can. Oh, not to discard it, surely? The next minute, she switched the magazine to her other hand, tossed the paper bag in the garbage, and left.

A few minutes later, the children came to the park, straight from school.

Oh, wonder where she is? Restlessly, they scanned the park, then just stood there, obviously at a loss. No doubt a park that has just the Woman in the Yellow Cardigan seated in it wasn't scintillating enough for them. After a while, they started playing rock-paper-scissors, but with none of the usual enthusiasm, and then, bereft of their usual playtime companion, they embarked on a game of safe-if-you're-high tag.

The next day, the Woman in the Purple Skirt headed out to an interview. It was for a job in a soap-making factory.

The Woman in the Purple Skirt had not got the hint at all.

Judging from past experience, if she passed the interview and got the job, this would mean that the soul-destroying daily grind would immediately begin. Every day she would be doing nothing but going back and forth between her apartment and her workplace. But if she didn't get the job, then she would once again be loitering around the neighborhood.

For the next week, and the week after that, the Woman in the Purple Skirt continued to hang around the neighborhood. Clearly, she hadn't got the job.

A few days later, the Woman in the Purple Skirt again headed out for a job interview. This time it was at a factory that made Chinese-style steamed pork buns. More evidence of her complete lack of judgment. Didn't she know that if you wanted to work in the food industry, the first thing they look at is the condition of your nails and hair? No way is a woman with dry, dull, unkempt hair like a rat's nest, and nails that are black, going to stand a chance. I knew she was going to fail—and of course that's exactly what happened.

On the same day as the interview for that job, she also went for another interview, at a different company. This one was for a "stock controller—night shift." I ask you: Why go for a job like that? I couldn't help feeling puzzled. Didn't she realize that on night shifts there are bound to be way more men than women? This is just a guess, but I get the feeling that the Woman in the Purple Skirt has an aversion to men. This is not to say she likes women or anything like that. But if you're working in an environment where you're surrounded by men, well, inevitably it takes its toll, doesn't it? But not to worry, because she didn't pass that interview either.

In the meantime, what with all this time wasting, the period the Woman in the Purple Skirt had spent out of work had reached a new record. It was now a good two months. Of course, this was only since I started keeping track. Any day now, surely, her savings were going to be depleted. Was she still managing to pay her rent on time—not to mention her electricity and gas bills? Wasn't her landlord going to start making preposterous demands, serving her with formal reminders, threatening to take her to court if she didn't pay up immediately, demanding that she find a cosigner even though the original contract had not required a guarantor? Because once you find yourself in that kind of position, I'm afraid it's a slippery slope. I'd say your only recourse is to stand your ground—and do so brazenly. That's certainly what I had done. Recently I had decided to stop wasting any more thought on how to pay my rent.

It had all started with that stupid collision with that butcher's display case. That's when things had begun to go wrong.

The fact was, coming up with the money for the payments for the repair bill had required that I withhold the monthly rent for my apartment, and I was now in arrears. I was still making a bit of extra income with the money I got from selling odds and ends at bazaars, but it was peanuts. With the dire state of my finances, paying both rent and repair bill was always going to be a nonstarter.

That said, I was still very preoccupied with finding ways I could escape from the debtors who I knew were going to come knocking at my door. I had investigated which coin lockers were in which train stations, with a view to transferring the few valuables I had left while I still could, before my landlord or one of his lawyers decided to make a forced entry into my apartment. I had identified a number of low-budget "capsule" hotels and manga coffee shops where I could take refuge if I had to make a quick getaway, and located a total of ten cheap boarding-houses, in this prefecture and the adjacent one, where I could lie low for a while. If it ever came to that, I would happily share this information with the Woman in the Purple Skirt, but it doesn't look as though we've quite got there yet.

As of now, I haven't seen any sign of threatening letters posted on the Woman in the Purple Skirt's apartment door. Nor have I noticed anyone who appears to be her landlord staking out her building, waiting and watching for her to come home. At night I see the lights go on in her place, and the dial on her gas meter appears to be steadily ticking over. She must be managing to pay her rent, and her electricity and heating bills.

It would seem, however, that her telephone has been cut off. A few weeks into her job search, the Woman in the Purple Skirt started going out to the pay phone in front of the convenience store to arrange job interviews.

When the Woman in the Purple Skirt goes to the convenience store, she never enters—she simply uses the pay phone outside. It falls to me to enter the store. I go right inside, head for the corner where the magazine stands are, take the latest issue of the jobs magazine, and then leave it for her to find on her Exclusively Reserved Seat.

The jobs magazine comes out on a weekly basis, unless it's a double issue. But don't assume the contents change just because there's a new cover every week. Workplaces that are continually short of staff place the same ad in every issue. While I didn't accompany her to every interview, the Woman in the Purple Skirt applied for a number of other jobs too, after that spate of attempts, and often in tandem. She didn't get any of them. Hardly surprising, considering the kinds of jobs she chose—all totally unsuitable. Telephone receptionist, shopping plaza floor guide, et cetera. Would you believe that she even applied to be a waitress? Why would anyone hire someone as a waitress in a café who is happy to drink straight from the water fountain in her local park? Clearly, the repeated rejections were affecting her mind. Needless to say, the café told her immediately to get lost.

And so, I am sorry to say, it was a good three

months before the Woman in the Purple Skirt finally had a telephone interview to work at a place that was willing to consider hiring her. During that time, I had visited the convenience store to collect the jobs magazine for her a good ten times.

It's possible that I was to blame for this having taken her so long. Maybe I should have done more than simply circle listings with a highlighter—maybe I should have dog-eared the pages, or added little sticky notes. I'm sure there were any number of things I could have done better, but never mind— eventually, the Woman in the Purple Skirt came to the right decision. One evening, I saw her leave her apartment and make a beeline for the pay phone outside the convenience store. I could see that she was holding a little scrap of paper tightly in her hand.

Clutching the receiver, her face taut, she nodded several times as she listened. "Yes . . . Yes . . . I understand." And then, "No . . . Yes . . . No, never."

She used a felt-tip marker to write something on her palm. Was it "3," perhaps, and then maybe "8"?

Definitely numbers. Three o'clock on the eighth? The date and time of the interview?

After she'd put down the receiver, her face remained tense. That didn't surprise me. Every single one of her interviews up till now had ended in failure. Who wouldn't be worried? But (not to get ahead of myself) this time, at this workplace, I was sure it was going to be different. This time, I could guarantee one hundred percent that she would get the job. Because this was a workplace where they were always short of workers. Basically, anyone who applied was going to be welcomed with open arms.

Even so, it would be good to go to this interview with, at the very least, a clean head of hair. She should trim her nails—and also apply a bit of lipstick, if she had such a thing. Because first impressions count, and little touches like those might make all the difference. Whenever I saw her, her hair was its usual mess—dull, dry, sticking out all over the place. I strongly suspected she was washing her hair with soap. I'd once had a part-time job at a shampoo factory, and I still had a fair number of shampoo

samples from the huge stash I'd managed to collect.
What about getting her to use some of my shampoo?

It was just after midday. I was standing at what
was pretty much the epicenter of the shopping district, holding a translucent plastic bag stuffed with
every shampoo sample I had. This was the spot
where TV camera crews conducted their street interviews. There were always throngs of people, since the
roads leading off the main shopping street, which
ran on an east–west axis, led to a large supermarket
on the right and a pachinko parlor on the left. Occasionally people handed out flyers there, but rarely
product samples. Shoppers and passersby gladly accepted the freebies I was offering. One or two of
them even took one, moved on, and then came back
for another. It was gratifying to see that my efforts
were being appreciated, but at this rate I was going to
be left with none for the person who needed them
most. To anyone who came back a second or third
time, I now simply shook my head and turned them
away.

When I was down to five of my little packets of

shampoo, the Woman in the Purple Skirt finally made an appearance in the shopping district.

Noticing me handing out free samples, she cast a curious glance at the contents of my plastic bag. But she didn't actually come over to me, and instead walked straight on by.

Just as I was swiveling myself around to follow her and press a sample into her hands, I felt somebody grab me by the elbow.

"Hey. Who are you? You're not from around here, are you? Have you got permission from the Shopkeepers Association?"

It was the proprietor of the Tatsumi sake store.

The Tatsumi sake store is the oldest of all the stores in the shopping district. Its proprietor is also the president of the local Shopping District Shopkeepers Association. Normally a courteous, smiling sort of man, he proceeded to grill me in a very unfriendly tone.

"Answer me. Come on! What are you handing out? What are those things? Let me have a look."

I shook my arm free of his grip.

"Hey! Oi! Wait!"

Normally, there is nothing I hate more than having to run, but this was one time I needed to. As I ran, I soon caught up with the Woman in the Purple Skirt, then left her far behind me. Once I'd made my way through the shopping district and was out on the main road, I kept running, repeatedly glancing over my shoulder, certain that the proprietor of the Tatsumi sake store was chasing after me. At a certain point, however, looking over my shoulder for the umpteenth time, I realized he was nowhere in sight.

Eventually—much later, after dark—I made a special excursion to the apartment of the Woman in the Purple Skirt and hung my bag of shampoo samples on her doorknob. This is probably what I should have done in the first place. I put my ear up against the door and heard a faint, steady scrubbing sound. It seemed she was brushing her teeth. Well, that was a good sign. If she kept this up, maybe she was even going to wash her hair.

Woman in the Purple Skirt! Give it your best shot! Get through the interview, and get the job!

FOUR DAYS LATER, THE OUTCOME OF THE JOB interview was clear. Whether it was all my fervent prayers that did the trick, or the "fresh floral"–scented shampoo I had given her, or because the company is so desperate that it would take anyone, the Woman in the Purple Skirt had got the job. It had been a long time coming, but finally, she had made it through. She was standing at the starting line.

First day at the new job. The Woman in the Purple Skirt left her apartment a little on the early side, at about 7:30 a.m., and headed to work. I was waiting for her at the bus stop. We got on the bus not far from the entrance to the shopping district, and got off near her place of work. For forty minutes we were being jolted around on the bus. It was 8:30 when the Woman in the Purple Skirt knocked on the door of her workplace.

When she entered the office, she was handed her corporate uniform and given a key to the locker room by the agency director. First, go and change. The Woman in the Purple Skirt did as she was told, and headed straight to the locker room, which was the next door down from the office.

The corporate uniform was a neat black dress. A good, sturdy garment, nicely "breathable," and also conveniently stain resistant (or rather, since it was black, the stains didn't show). Made of polyester, it dried within minutes of washing—which was also convenient. Perhaps the one unattractive feature was that the fabric generated a lot of static. A minor problem, but annoying nevertheless.

With the black uniform, she wore matching black shoes that she bought yesterday in the shopping district. But oh dear, as soon as she tried to step into her new black tights, also purchased yesterday, at the hundred-yen store, there was a ripping sound. The Woman in the Purple Skirt took off the tights and discarded them, then slipped her feet straight into her shoes: she would go bare legged. The finishing touch was a white apron. But oh, the Woman in the Purple Skirt had managed to tie the apron in the wrong way. She was supposed to pull the ties over her shoulders and cross them before securing them.

Now in her work uniform, the Woman in the Purple Skirt knocked again on the office door. By now a few more people were in the room.

The agency director was sitting at his desk, staring at his computer screen. When the Woman in the Purple Skirt entered the office, the director lifted his eyes, glanced at her face, and then glanced at her legs.

Maybe he didn't realize she wasn't wearing stockings. In any case, he didn't say anything about that. But he did point out that she had tied her apron wrong.

"Tsukada-san, Tsukada-san." He beckoned to Supervisor Tsukada, who was standing next to the office whiteboard. "See to her, would you," the director said, and gestured toward the Woman in the Purple Skirt.

"Yup. One second." Supervisor Tsukada put down

the nameplate she was holding and walked over to the Woman in the Purple Skirt.

"First day?" And she rested her hands lightly on the Woman in the Purple Skirt's shoulders. It was the first time I had ever seen anyone apart from the children in the park touch the Woman in the Purple Skirt.

"Yes," came the reply, spoken in a tiny voice.

Supervisor Tsukada rotated the Woman in the Purple Skirt so she was facing the other way. With quick movements, she undid the bow at the waist, unbuttoned the ties, and, jostling her roughly, rearranged the ties. She crossed them over each other, buttoned them, and then retied them in a bow.

"Good grief, aren't you a skinny little thing! Did you eat breakfast this morning?"

"Yes," the Woman in the Purple Skirt replied. Again, her voice was barely audible. Really? What could she have eaten? I wondered.

"What did you have?" Supervisor Tsukada demanded.

"Cornflakes," replied the Woman in the Purple Skirt.

"Cornflakes? You won't be able to do much work on that! A good breakfast is rice! Rice! You got that?"

Supervisor Tsukada gave the Woman in the Purple Skirt a little tap on the shoulder. Again, she replied with a "Yes," in the same small voice. And then she gave a demure little giggle.

For a moment, I thought I had misheard. But no, it was definitely her. Amazingly, the Woman in the Purple Skirt had just let out an ingratiating laugh.

IT WAS 9:00 A.M. THE USUAL MORNING MEETING got underway. Since today was the first Monday of the month, the manager from the hotel was present. After everyone stood and wished one another a good morning, he said a few words directing us to "continue with the initiative begun last month to keep strict tabs on the complimentary items provided for guests." And then he left.

This manager had a distinctly laissez-faire attitude when it came to giving direction to the service companies working for the hotel. His policy was basically to stay out of it. This was why he turned up only once a month for the morning meetings, and also why, even now, he didn't know the names of any of the staff. It was only recently that he had started telling us we needed to keep a tighter check on the complimentary items—previously he hadn't bothered even to cast his eye over the checklists. Everybody thought he was an arrogant twerp—standing there, head thrown back, barking out his orders—especially considering he was never around anyway.

Once the hotel manager had made his quick exit, it was the turn of the agency director, who stood up and read from a list of prepared topics. These included today's room occupancy rate and the mottoes to bear in mind this month. There were too many of us to be able to fit into the office for morning meetings, so some of us were always left standing in the corridor between the office and the hotel.

Sadly, from where I stood, I couldn't get a view of the Woman in the Purple Skirt. Not so much because of the number of people but because of the rotund figure of the agency director, who stood like a blank wall right in front of her. The Woman in the Purple Skirt was completely obscured.

The director next read out a list of yesterday's oversights.

"Room 215: Mirror not wiped. Room 308: Kettle not filled with water. Room 502: New roll of toilet paper did not have the end folded into a neat triangle for the next guest. Now, I repeat: Make sure you give a thorough last check before you leave any room, using the so-called point-and-call routine. You know the one. Direct your eyes to parts of the room, point your finger at each item, and say it out loud. That usually prevents most mistakes."

Everybody listened—or pretended to listen—to what he was saying, with solemn expressions on their faces.

"And last of all, I want you to meet our newest recruit. She'll be working with us starting today."

And here, he glanced behind him, and stepped back.

"Now. Please introduce yourself."

At last. The Woman in the Purple Skirt's face came into view, or at least a glimpse of it. Perhaps on someone's advice, the Woman in the Purple Skirt seemed to have gathered into a tight ponytail the hair that normally hung loosely over her shoulders. The style showed off her oval-shaped face, and she looked surprisingly clean and neat.

"Come. Introduce yourself." The director motioned for her to come forward. The Woman in the Purple Skirt did as she was told. But then she simply froze.

"Well, come on . . . introduce yourself," the director whispered to her, frowning. "Just say your name. You do have a name, don't you?"

There were some titters of laughter.

". . . My last name is Hino. . . ."

Finally, she had uttered her own name, just barely managing to force it out.

"And what's your first name?"

". . . Mayuko . . ."

What did she say? the cleaning staff asked loudly. I didn't catch it. . . . Did you hear it? No! Did you? No, not one word of it. Sorry! Hey, speak up a little, will you? Can't hear you!

The truth was, she was perfectly audible. "My last name is Hino. My full name is Mayuko Hino!" she had said, quite distinctly. And then: "And I have another name too. The Woman in the Purple Skirt!" That part was very audible, at least to the Woman in the Yellow Cardigan.

"Hey, speak up, will you? Can you say that again, please?!"

"Her name is Mayuko Hino-san!" The director's voice boomed out, taking over. And then, on her behalf: "It's a pleasure to meet you!"

THE JOB OF THE AGENCY DIRECTOR SEEMS almost impossible. He has to assemble the staff, negotiate with the hotel, collect staff reports, produce bulletins, help out on-site if there are staff shortages, schedule the shifts, deal with the objections that inevitably arise from someone or other on the staff . . . He must find himself continually pulled between the head office and the hotel. And then, on top of it all, rumor has it that at home he's a henpecked husband. He has to do exactly as his wife tells him.

That must be partly why he is packing on weight. It must be all the stress. These days all he seems to get from the head office is one stern directive after another. "Do not—whatever happens—lose any more staff! We're hard pressed enough as it is!"

As soon as the Woman in the Purple Skirt's self-introduction was over, the director told her to come to the office during her lunch break—he would give her some voice training. The Woman in the Purple Skirt nodded, though she looked a bit anxious. In fact, it is not unusual for employees on their first day of work at this company to be made to do voice drills in the required daily greetings and exhortations. The place where it happens is always the same: outside, in the recycling-collection area.

We were in the recycling-collection area. The sanitation workers had not yet come to pick up the trash. Other than the director and the Woman in the Purple Skirt, no one else was there.

"Standing where you are, just try shouting as loud as you can."

The director had positioned the Woman in the Purple Skirt next to the crates holding recyclable bottles, cans, glass, and newspapers. He himself took up a place by the large dumpster for general recyclable waste. The two of them stood on opposite sides of the service bay, facing each other as if in a standoff.

The lesson took the form of a series of drills. The

director started each drill with a brief vocal exercise used by actors based on the sounds of the hiragana alphabet, to limber up the voice.

At first, I couldn't hear the voice of the Woman in the Purple Skirt at all.

"*A—e—i—u—e—o—a—o!*" the director beeped in staccato fashion. And then: "*Ohayo gozaimasu!* Good morning!"

The director's words rang out unanswered in the collection area.

"*Ta—te—chi—tsu—te—to—ta—to! Arigato gozaimasu!* Thank you! We appreciate your kindness!"

In college, the director had belonged to a student acting club. Everyone knew about it. At one time, the story went, he had even thought about becoming a professional actor. I suspected he had other motivations, like a relationship with an actress, because he hadn't stuck with it for even two years before giving up altogether on the idea of acting. Still, his voice was unusually resonant: only someone with some stage experience could project like that. No doubt his big tub of a belly helped.

"*Na—ne—ni—nu—ne—no—na—no! Otsukare-sama desu!* Good work!"

Perhaps encouraged by his enthusiasm, the Woman in the Purple Skirt started to answer him. Her voice grew steadily louder and clearer.

"*Arigato gozaimasu!*"

"*Arigato gozaimasu!*"

"*Itte irasshaimase!* See you again soon!"

"*Itte irasshaimase!*"

"That's more like it! *Itte irasshaimase!*"

"*Itte irasshaimase!*"

"*Otsukare-sama desu!*"

"*Otsukare-sama desu!*"

"That's the way!"

The director went on to explain to the Woman in the Purple Skirt that the greetings and exhortations she would have to use would fall into two broad categories—those for greeting a guest in the hotel corridor, or a colleague at the cleaning agency. Being able to offer the right kind of greeting or exhortation, in the appropriate tone of voice, is essential for anyone who wants to be considered an adult. But you'd be amazed by how many people just can't seem to manage it. This is one of the reasons the agency is constantly short of staff. The more experienced staff take every opportunity to persecute any new recruits who can't get the hang of it, until the recruits eventually quit. If the fault lies with anybody, it has to be with the ones who do the persecuting, but, well, if you're an adult and you can't even manage a "Hello" in the morning, you have to wonder. . . . But then again, I'm hardly the world's most socially adept person.

"Now, one more time. A bit louder. *Arigato gozaimasu!*"

"*Arigato gozaimasu!*"

"A touch more energy. *Arigato gozaimasu!*"

"*Arigato gozaimasu!*"

"Louder. Loud enough so that the person over there—whoever it is—lurking in the smoking area can hear you. *Arigato gozaimasu!*"

"*Arigato gozaimasu!*"

"Hey, you! Yes, you, whoever you are. Your face is kind of in the shadows, but I can see you're wearing our uniform. Yes, you, standing right there. Raise your hand and wave if you can hear her. Here we go, then: *Arigato gozaimasu!*"

"*Arigato gozaimasu!*"

I raised my hand and gave a little wave.

"Well, that person seems to have heard you. Excellent. You've passed!"

THANKS TO THE CRASH COURSE GIVEN TO HER by the director, that afternoon the Woman in the Purple Skirt was being treated by the regular members of the cleaning staff like an altogether different person. Perhaps it was just the stark contrast with the appalling impression she had made with her self-introduction in the morning, but now all she had to do was call out a clear *"Otsukare-sama desu!"* and give a little bow with her head when anyone stepped into the elevator, and all of them would look utterly amazed.

"Wait, what? So she can talk after all, and like normal!"

"She actually looks as if she might have some wits about her!"

This reaction relieved me of my first worry. At least now she wouldn't be persecuted for not even being able to properly recite the various obligatory salutations and exhortations. More than a few of the older cleaning staff, and managers like Supervisor Tsukada and Supervisor Hamamoto, made it a policy to refuse to deal with new recruits who couldn't handle this most basic of requirements. I didn't know how many new employees I'd seen quit before finding out even the first thing about the job.

But the Woman in the Purple Skirt had mastered this part. Her induction started that very afternoon, in a room in the hotel's utility corridor.

Supervisor Tsukada began with a demonstration of the various pieces of housekeeping equipment, and then handed the Woman in the Purple Skirt a form, telling her to fill in the blanks with the names of the items.

But, oh dear, the Woman in the Purple Skirt didn't have a pen.

"You mean you forgot?" asked Supervisor Tsukada in stern surprise. "The least you can do is bring a pen with you to work."

"I'm sorry." The Woman in the Purple Skirt hung her head.

"Well, what about a notebook?"

The Woman in the Purple Skirt shook her head. Supervisor Tsukada took out an unused notebook from the tote bag she carried around with her.

"I'll give you this one."

"Is it all right? It's yours, isn't it?"

"Of course. I've got lots more. I bought five in a special deal."

"Thank you! I appreciate your kindness!" More evidence of the efficacy of the director's vocal coaching.

"Now. The one thing you have to understand about this job," Supervisor Tsukada said as she handed her a pen, "is that it's rather mindless. Basically, you're doing the same thing over and over again. Anyone can do it, once they get used to it. It's actually quite simple."

"Yes." The Woman in the Purple Skirt opened the notebook she'd been given, and wrote: "Involves doing the same thing over and over again."

"Good grief!" Supervisor Tsukada exclaimed, taking a quick peek at her notes. "I hope you're not going to write down everything I say!" And she laughed boisterously, giving the Woman in the Purple Skirt a whack on the shoulder.

The Woman in the Purple Skirt was now assigned to the training floor, which was, as the name implied, the floor specifically for trainees. Here, she would be joined by Supervisor Tsukada, whose specific job was to train the trainees, as well as three other supervisors who would come in one by one to observe, and ten or so fledgling members of the staff, all of whom had joined within the last year. She would have her cleaning procedures strictly monitored, until such time as Supervisor Tsukada stamped her official seal on a document that would signify she had completed her training.

The director also dropped in to see how his protégée was doing. The Woman in the Purple Skirt happened to be out of earshot, having been pulled aside by one of the supervisors to learn how to replenish the cleaning fluid in the housekeeping cart.

"The new girl looks like she'll be all right," Supervisor Tsukada told the director.

"Is she able to communicate?" the director asked.

"Uh-huh. Her responses are just as they should be."

"Ah. Good." The director nodded, looking pleased. "My voice lessons must have done the trick."

"She is quiet and reserved, so at first I doubted whether she would be up to the job. But so far she's been doing everything exactly as I tell her to. She's very conscientious. And she's quick and nimble, despite her dopey manner."

"Really!"

"I asked her if she had ever played any sports. Apparently, she used to be on the athletics squad. For six years, all the way up through junior high and high school."

"I see!"

"Yes, apparently she excelled at short-distance running. It just shows you, doesn't it? You should never judge someone by the way they look. Well, thank goodness for that. We've finally managed to get someone capable!"

So it turns out the Woman in the Purple Skirt

really is speedy and agile and fit after all. I found that hard to believe. On the athletics squad? And for six years?

And what was all this about her being "conscientious" and "capable"? That set me on edge. Did it mean she had failed over and over in all those job interviews just because of her physical appearance? I would never have described her as "spruce," not by any standard, but how very odd that all it took was for her to put on a uniform like everyone else, and tie her hair back in a ponytail, to all of a sudden start being thought of as "capable." Truth be told, since the morning, every time the Woman in the Purple Skirt passed in front of me, I was quite certain I had caught a whiff of that "fresh floral" fragrance. She must have used one of the shampoo samples I had hung on her doorknob. They do say that certain fragrances can have a positive effect on mood and emotion. I was sure that what had really won over the management was the smell of my shampoo.

At the end of the first day, Supervisor Tsukada

gave the Woman in the Purple Skirt an apple. It was a big red one.

"This is a *hokuto* apple. Very expensive." Supervisor Tsukada put a finger to her lips and said, "Shh!"

The Woman in the Purple Skirt took the apple with both hands. "Really? Is it okay if I take it?"

"Of course."

"But doesn't it belong to . . . ?"

"Oh, it's fine. Come on. Everybody does it. Even me. Look."

Supervisor Tsukada pointed at each of her breasts. They stuck out unnaturally, perfectly round and much bigger than usual. If you looked carefully, the shape of each was slightly different. The right breast was an apple, and the left breast, slightly smaller, was an orange. Supervisor Tsukada then plunged her hand into the pocket of her apron and revealed the tip of a banana.

The Woman in the Purple Skirt let out a little laugh. That same ingratiating chuckle.

"Well, they are only going to be thrown away otherwise. It's a waste." Then, addressing Supervisor Hamamoto and Supervisor Tachibana, she said:

"It's fine. Isn't it, you two?"

They nodded.

"Absolutely."

"No housewife worth her salt would allow food that's still edible to be thrown away. Unforgivable."

Supervisor Hamamoto and Supervisor Tachibana each brought out what they were carrying in their tote bags to show the Woman in the Purple Skirt: a green *orin* apple and an orange, and an orange and a banana. These were all leftovers from the supply of fruit that the hotel provided for guests.

"If anyone says anything, you can say housekeeping had already disposed of it."

"That's right."

"Just make sure the director doesn't see." Supervisor Tsukada again put a finger to her lips and said, "Shh!"

"Don't worry about it, nobody will say a thing," interjected Supervisor Hamamoto. She pointed at

Supervisor Tachibana. "I mean, look at her. It's an open secret that she fills her water bottle with the champagne that guests leave behind. And no one in charge has ever found out!"

"Is that true?" the Woman in the Purple Skirt asked politely, looking shocked.

"Of course not! She's just making it up!" Supervisor Tachibana waved a hand in front of her face, laughing.

"Oh, it's true all right! You see that blue water bottle she carries around? It's got champagne in it! You just watch: she'll take a sip from it, and then— *mmm tum-tum-tum*—smack her lips!"

"Oh stop! It's not true," protested Supervisor Tachibana.

There was a suppressed snort, followed by an outright laugh, from the Woman in the Purple Skirt. This time it wasn't just polite laughter. For the first time I heard the Woman in the Purple Skirt laugh and really mean it.

"Would you like to take this home?" Supervisor Tsukada asked the Woman in the Purple Skirt, holding out an orange that she'd pulled out of the pocket of her dress.

"Is it all right? Is that allowed?"

"Of course! Haven't I made that clear? Each of us has already taken one orange anyway."

"But what about . . ." For some reason the Woman in the Purple Skirt seemed to feel she shouldn't. She glanced quickly at someone else, standing a little way away, behind Supervisor Tsukada. Supervisor Tsukada followed her eyes.

"O-oh. Don't worry about *her*. It's fine. She hates fruit."

"Is that true?"

"Of course it is. Right, Supervisor Gondo?"

"Well, if it really is all right. Thank you. I will take the orange," the Woman in the Purple Skirt said, and gave a little bob of her head.

The Woman in the Purple Skirt took the apple and the orange offered to her by Supervisor Tsukada, hid them in the folds of her black dress, and headed to the locker room to change. Walking past the office, she leaned forward and called out, *"Otsukare-sama desu!*" like the embodiment of the dutiful new recruit. The regular staff members, apparently forgetting all their scorn at the morning meeting, called out the required exhortations. "Good work today!" "Give it your best tomorrow too!"

IT WAS THE WOMAN IN THE PURPLE SKIRT'S
second day at work. Today she took the 8:02 bus, the
one after the bus she took the day before. During the
week, the bus comes every twenty minutes. The earlier bus gets you in with too much time to spare before the morning meeting. But the later one means
you end up arriving late for work. The Woman in
the Purple Skirt took the middle one, and punched
in at 8:52.

This morning the Woman in the Purple Skirt
delivered her greetings in a ringing voice. *"Ohayo
gozaimasu!"* she called out when she entered the office. And again, when she opened the door to the
locker room: *"Ohayo gozaimasu!"*

The director and other members of the staff
glanced up. *"Ohayo!"* they replied. An approving
little smile appeared on the face of the director, who

was no doubt pleased with how effective his coaching had been.

Some of the staff asked her how she was today—whether her body was stiff or sore anywhere. "No!" she replied cheerfully. "I'm quite all right!" For my part I knew for a fact that every muscle of hers must be aching. Her shoulders, her arms, her hips, her legs. As she waited for the bus, I had seen her tilt her neck from side to side till her vertebrae popped, a little frown on her face.

Today, day two, the Woman in the Purple Skirt changed quickly into her work uniform. Yesterday she had taken quite a lot of time, but today she seemed to have it all down pat. It looked like she had put on her tights at home. The ties of her apron were drawn over her shoulders in a neat X across her back, without a single twist.

Looking at herself in the mirror on the inside of the locker door, the Woman in the Purple Skirt began brushing her hair. I noticed the brush she was using had the hotel logo on the handle. Yesterday Supervisor Tsukada had told her to take anything she fancied from the hotel amenities, and she had picked out this hairbrush as well as some cotton swabs. Every stroke of the brush sent a strong gust of "fresh floral" fragrance wafting into my nostrils.

Just before she left the locker room, the Woman in the Purple Skirt did some simple stretches. Grunting softly, she executed a few knee bends and a few rolls of her shoulder blades. It actually looked as if she were in quite a bit of pain. I knew that it wasn't just her work at the hotel that was to blame. The truth was that after work, the Woman in the Purple Skirt had spent a full ninety minutes literally running around.

Yesterday, just under half the hotel rooms were booked. Having punched out at 3:30 p.m., the Woman in the Purple Skirt boarded the 3:53 bus and arrived back in her neighborhood at just past 4:30. Whenever the Woman in the Purple Skirt had got off work early before, she would go straight home. But yesterday, in an unusual break with precedent, she dropped by the park.

Upon taking her Exclusively Reserved Seat, the

Woman in the Purple Skirt reached inside the tote bag on her lap and took out a large, bright red apple—the apple that Supervisor Tsukada had given her. She brought it up to her face, opened her mouth wide, and took a large bite.

Immediately she took another bite, and then another one. Three bites in quick succession. She was about to take a fourth bite when some children called out from beyond the fence. "Hey! There she is!" "She's eating an apple!" Suddenly there they were, laughing and pointing at her. With a chorus of whoops, they hopped over the metal wicket gates at the park's entrance. Forming a circle not too far from her bench, they started cheerfully playing rock-paper-scissors. For three rounds, the game ended in a tie, and on the fourth round someone who'd thrown out scissors lost. "Aw! Son of a bitch!" he cursed, looking upset, of course, but also, predictably, rather pleased. He trotted up to the Woman in the Purple Skirt, arm raised.

Wham! The impact as he brought his hand down on the Woman in the Purple Skirt's shoulder knocked the apple out of her grasp, and it fell to the ground.

The boy let out a little cry, and turned pale. Surely he should have known this would happen if he hit her so hard? The boy stared at the apple as it rolled along the ground, and the other children too stared.

The apple rolled right up to the garbage can, where it finally came to a standstill. The leader, the one who had whacked the Woman in the Purple Skirt, seemed to return to his senses, and ran after it. He picked up the apple, which now had some dirt on it, and brought it back to her with a look of apology on his face.

"Sorry." The boy held out the apple to her, timidly.

Immediately the other children, all of whom had been looking on, ran up to the Woman in the Purple Skirt, one after another, and stood before her, heads bowed. Sorry! We didn't mean it! Truly, we are very sorry! We apologize! We made a mistake! So sorry!

The sight of all the children, heads bobbing, was so bizarre, I half thought they were starting another of their games.

But I was wrong. That wasn't the case at all. The children were apologizing from the bottom of their hearts. The eyes of the boy who had whacked her were even pooling with tears.

"It's quite all right!" The Woman in the Purple Skirt waved her hand slightly in front of her breast to show no hard feelings.

It's quite all right! Had she really said that? The surprise of it seemed to stun the children.

She actually said something!

Yeah, amazing, isn't it?

The children exchanged glances, and looked curiously at the Woman in the Purple Skirt.

"I'll go and wash it!" The boy who had whacked her dashed off toward the water fountain. And the other children ran off after him.

"You don't have to do that. It's quite all right!" The Woman in the Purple Skirt stood up from her bench and went over to the water fountain.

Together the children washed the apple meticulously, passing it one to the other, each taking it in turn. Finally, the apple, now washed absolutely clean, was pressed into the hands of the Woman in the Purple Skirt. When she returned to her seat, the children followed, gathering around her. Then she took a bite of the apple.

"It tastes good." The Woman in the Purple Skirt handed it to a boy who stood next to her. The boy who had whacked her on the shoulder. After taking a bite, he announced: "It does taste good." He then passed the apple to the girl standing next to him. She too took a bite, and then passed it on to another girl, who was standing next to her.

"It tastes good."

"So sweet."

"And juicy."

"It's delicious."

Round and round the apple went, counterclockwise, with the Woman in the Purple Skirt standing in the middle of the children. One boy took a bite, and then a girl took a bite next to his, and then another girl next to her bite, and then a boy next to hers, and another boy next to his, and yet another boy took a bite out of the place next to his, and then the

Woman in the Purple Skirt took a bite next to the place he had bitten into. After two rounds of this, the apple was reduced to its core.

Once they had finished the apple, the Woman in the Purple Skirt and the children began to play a game of tag. This was the first time the Woman in the Purple Skirt had ever been made a member of the children's little gang. The game of tag continued on and on, till well after nightfall, and each and every one of them had a go at being "it."

The Woman in the Purple Skirt was the last one to be "it."

Scattering all over the park, the children ran hither and thither like little mice, their darting, unpredictable movements keeping them easily out of reach. Even for someone like her, with her background in competitive sports, it seemed impossible to catch them. Round and round she went for a while, trying her very best to tag them, looking as if she were putting her heart and soul into it, but then, at a certain point, unaccountably, she suddenly stopped running.

Turning her back on the children as they darted around her, the Woman in the Purple Skirt started looking at the flower beds, then cast a glance up at the park's clock and walked very slowly all around, as if she were taking a stroll. Something wasn't right, the children realized, and they ran up to her with expressions of concern. I too was concerned. What on earth could have happened?

"What's the matter?" asked one, peering up inquiringly into her face.

"Are you mad at us?"

The Woman in the Purple Skirt let out a sigh. "I'm so tired."

"You're tired?"

"Are you all right?"

"Would you like to take a break?" a little boy asked her, standing right in front of her.

And then—

She gave him a sharp tap on the shoulder. "Haha! Gotcha! You're 'it'!" she cried with a huge smile on her face.

Auuugh! It was a trick! The children all squealed

and laughed and clapped their hands. Quite the player, aren't you? You had us completely fooled! The children gave the Woman in the Purple Skirt pats of congratulation on her shoulders and back. With every pat, clouds of dust rose into the air and wafted on the night breeze all the way over to me as I sat on the bench closest to the park's entrance.

A few minutes later, the park was deserted. I spotted a single orange underneath the Exclusively Reserved Seat. I picked it up and sank my teeth straight into it, not even bothering to peel it. *Chomp, chomp, chomp, chomp.* Just like they'd done with the apple. I didn't actually reach the flesh of the orange on my first bite, but I carried on guzzling, and gradually the juice started to fill up my mouth and drench my chin.

I gave myself over to chomping the orange. All that watching from a distance had left me parched.

BUT OF COURSE THE WOMAN IN THE PURPLE Skirt could hardly take today off for being sore all over from too much tag. So her second day at work was just as exacting as her first, and she started her training first thing in the morning.

Every so often, I would hear Supervisor Tsukada through the door, which was left open, saying to her: "Well, this is a secret, but how about . . ." It seemed some sort of person-to-person transfer was taking place of the tips and tricks for cleaning rooms quickly without exerting too much effort. As someone who made no bones about refusing to teach anyone she considered a shirker, Supervisor Tsukada evidently thought highly of the Woman in the Purple Skirt, who hung on her every word and wrote down in her notebook even the most trivial bit of advice. At this rate, I could see her completing her training within a month. Once that happened, she would be working on her own much more, making it easier for me to get to talk to her face-to-face—certainly easier than it was now, when she was working among all these people.

Today, yet again, I managed to miss the opportunity to introduce myself.

I'd had one chance in the final few minutes before the afternoon shift. She was alone in the cafeteria, enjoying a cup of tea. Just as I was working up the courage to go up to her, the director appeared and sat down next to her—right where I was hoping to sit.

"How are you finding everything? Do you think you'll stay?" I heard him ask her, evidently taking an interest in how the new employee was coming along.

"Yes! I am doing quite all right!" the Woman in the Purple Skirt answered with a smile.

"Ah, good. Between you and me, I was concerned that the supervisors might be bullying you." He lowered his voice as he said this last part.

"Everybody's being very kind," the Woman in the Purple Skirt replied.

"Hm. I hope that's the case. It's a motley crew we've got here. Especially those supervisors. Some of them are very eccentric. Wouldn't you agree?"

"Er . . . Um. Well . . ."

"Take Tsukada-san, for example . . ."

"Er . . . Um . . ." And she gave a little giggle.

"Hamamoto-san's pretty weird. And Tachibana-san, and Shinjo-san, Hori-san, Miyaji-san . . . Not forgetting Nakaya-san, or Okita-san. Nonomura-san . . . Every one of them is an oddball, frankly. Very fierce, all of them."

"Fierce . . . ?" Another little giggle.

"It's like a zoo."

"Oh, that's going too far. . . ." Again she emitted a giggle—slightly longer this time.

"Have you managed to remember who everyone is?"

"You mean the supervisors? Em, well, actually, no. . . ."

"I see. Well, I suppose they change every day, don't they, except for Supervisor Tsukada. It won't be long before you know them by name."

"Yes."

"But that makes me feel better. It's not unusual for girls who can't fit in, you know, to quit almost immediately. But you, Hino-san, you seem like you'll be able to fit in very well. I mean, my gosh, if Supervisor Tsukada already likes you, then you've got to be doing something right!"

"Supervisor Tsukada is very kind."

"She'd be pleased to hear you say that. Uh-oh. Time to get back to work."

The director got up from his chair, went to the vending machine, bought two cans of hot coffee, and came back.

"This one's for you."

"Are you sure?"

"To keep your strength up for this afternoon."

"Oh. I appreciate it, very much!"

"Ha ha. That's the reply I want to hear! Excellent!"

THE NEXT DAY WAS MY DAY OFF. BUT SINCE the Woman in the Purple Skirt was going in, I too decided to go in. She boarded the same bus as the day before, and punched in at exactly the same time. I was about to follow her, almost automatically, when something suddenly occurred to me and I returned my time card to the rack.

Although I had come in, I had not the slightest intention of doing any work. More to the point, it was my day off, so I wouldn't even have been included in the head count. In that case, then, why was I there? Well, naturally, it was to observe, from some concealed position, how hard she was working. And of course, if the right moment presented itself, I was also hoping to introduce myself.

But the moment I stepped inside the locker room, I realized I had made a catastrophic mistake.

Incredibly, I had forgotten my uniform. I'd have

no hope of gaining access to the floors of the hotel without it. Yesterday, as I always did the evening before my day off, I had brought the whole set, dress and apron, back with me, and this morning I had put it in the washing machine and then hung it out to dry on my veranda.

How stupid of me. I could hardly loiter in the hotel corridors in my ordinary clothes, and if I was going to borrow a uniform, that meant having to go and make conversation with whoever happened to be managing the front office. As soon as they realized it was my day off, I was pretty sure I'd be sent packing.

Feeling enraged and frustrated, I left the building, even though I'd only just arrived, then boarded a bus and returned home. Well, at least I'd had my season pass; I hadn't wasted any money. Such were my thoughts on the ride back.

Once home, I watched a little TV, then took a nap. When I woke up, I could see that it was already beginning to get dark. I stayed in bed a bit longer

and then, just before the stores in the shopping district would be closing, I roused myself and got up.

Once I was in the shopping district, I wandered
by the greengrocer's, then the drugstore, then the
hundred-yen shop, and took a look inside. At the Tatsumi sake store, I bought something from the vending machine at the entrance—avoiding actually
entering the shop itself. My last stop was the *sozaiya*,
the mom-and-pop shop that sold rice balls, ingredi-
ents for *oden*, and other basic prepared foods. I was
comparing two packs of something that had been
discounted, unable to decide which to buy, when I
raised my eyes and saw the Woman in the Purple
Skirt heading toward me.

I was stunned, never imagining we'd run into
each other at this time of day. I was sure I'd seen the
whiteboard show an occupancy rate at the hotel of
less than one third, in which case she would have
finished work hours ago and would already be en-
sconced at home.

The distance between us was a good fifty feet or

so. As I watched her walking up the street, something about her struck me as a bit off. She had none of the easy rhythm and speed that she normally had when walking through the shopping district. Maybe it was because it was late, and there were fewer people to avoid, but my goodness, she hardly seemed able to put one foot in front of the other.

Had Supervisor Tsukada worked her too hard? It was her third day of work. The closer she came, the more clearly I could see her face: her eyes were dull and unfocused, her head lolled on her neck, and her jaw was slack.

What could it be? What on earth could have happened to her?

I bitterly regretted how I had spent my morning. Why did I turn on the TV like that and just lie around napping and doing nothing? Why didn't I return to the hotel? I should have just shoved my uniform—who cared if it was damp—in my bag and gone straight back. I had my commuter pass. I shouldn't even have had to think about it.

Every now and then one of her legs seemed to

give way, and the Woman in the Purple Skirt staggered sideways. If somebody had tried to bump into her, she would've been sent flying and landed flat on her face. The thought crossed my mind, momentarily, but of course nobody tried anything so stupid. The Woman in the Purple Skirt passed right by me, slowly, and continued walking, or rather staggering, in the direction of her apartment.

After she had passed by me, a customer standing nearby remarked to the shop owner:

"That girl looked very unsteady. I wonder whether she'll be okay."

The owner threw a glance at the receding figure of the Woman in the Purple Skirt. "Well, she's able to walk. I don't think there's any cause for concern."

Neither of them appeared to be aware of who it was that had just passed by.

I spent the next day in a state of anxiety.

It was the Woman in the Purple Skirt's day off—her first since the day (Monday) she joined the agency. From the state she had been in the night before, I imagined she'd probably spend the whole day in bed. It was unlikely that someone so thoroughly inebriated could recover in the space of a single day. I wanted to ask Supervisor Tsukada what could have happened, but unusually, Supervisor Tsukada too was off that day.

What made me particularly concerned was the possibility that the Woman in the Purple Skirt wouldn't make it to work the morning after her day off. So many recruits stick it out for the first two or three days, and then, on their very first day off, all of sudden they just disappear.

I didn't want that to happen with the Woman in the Purple Skirt. Here she was, finally employed. She should stick it out just a little longer. At least until we got to know each other.

I felt considerable relief when I saw her the next morning at the front of the line for the bus.

Her demeanor was completely different from that of a couple of nights earlier. Her color had returned, and she was standing up straight, clear-eyed and focused.

When the bus came, it was already packed. It's

always like this in the morning, which is a pain in the neck, but waiting for the next bus would mean being late to work. Taking advantage of her small frame, the Woman in the Purple Skirt squeezed herself on board, pressing herself right up against the flank of a salaryman.

Several people in line for the bus gave up trying to squeeze on board and headed for the taxi stand, so I suddenly found myself near the front of the line, even though I had been toward the back. Like the Woman in the Purple Skirt, I scrunched down and then pushed my way in, pressing myself right up against the backpack of a high school student.

Inside the bus, the Woman in the Purple Skirt was completely obscured by clumps of salarymen. From where I stood, I could catch a glimpse of only a portion of her head and her shoulder. One of the men was having a good sniff of the Woman in the Purple Skirt's hair. She must still be using my "fresh floral"–scented shampoo. Maybe she'd washed her hair that very morning. Any day now, surely, she was going to run out of those samples. And what would happen then? Was her hair going to go back to being all dry and stiff again? She wouldn't get anyone sniffing her hair then.

For a moment, a gap appeared around her head, and I managed to get an unimpeded view of her face. "Oh! Hello! So you take this bus too?" Would I ever get to say that to her? Would she ever say it to me?

But something else had caught my attention. From where I stood, unable to move, I spotted a grain of rice stuck to her coat. It was on her right shoulder.

It appeared to be a cooked grain of rice that was now quite dry and hard. Supervisor Tsukada had told her that she should eat a traditional Japanese breakfast; maybe she was now doing so. For all I knew, the piece of rice could have been stuck on her shoulder for days. I wanted to pick it off for her. But pressed up against all these people, I could hardly move my hand, let alone my fingers.

Inch by inch, as stealthily as I could, I stretched out my arm toward that grain of rice. But just as my fingertips were about to pick it off her coat, the bus leaned into a series of steep curves and lurched violently, first one way and then the other. Rather than picking off the grain of rice, my fingers ended up tweaking the Woman in the Purple Skirt's nose.

The Woman in the Purple Skirt let out an odd sound.

"Ngha—!"

As quickly as I could, I withdrew my hand.

At the next stop, a whole load of passengers started to file off the bus, and I could now see that the Woman in the Purple Skirt had a fearful expression on her face and was looking searchingly at all the people around her. She must've been thinking: Somebody just tweaked me on the nose; which one of these people was it? Now she was glaring straight at me, with that same accusing look in her eyes. "It was you, wasn't it?" But no, the next second she went straight up to the man next to me—a salaryman, judging by his gray suit.

"You just touched my bottom, didn't you!" she said.

And then, pointing straight at him, she declared: "This man just groped me!"

The man started babbling incomprehensibly, clearly upset. But he did not deny it.

The other passengers immediately pushed forward and formed a tight ring around him.

The driver, seemingly aware of what was happening, came to an emergency stop in front of the first police box he saw.

The doors of the bus opened, and the Woman in the Purple Skirt quickly got out. The man was dragged out by the other passengers. Then the doors closed, and the bus continued on its way. From the rear window, I watched as a policeman emerged from the police box. The Woman in the Purple Skirt was handing over the man she suspected of touching her.

And so that day the Woman in the Purple Skirt arrived two hours late to work. After the morning meeting, the staff were abuzz as they waited for the elevator to take them to the hotel floors. Well, that didn't take long, did it—for her to go AWOL. Don't expect we'll see her again.

Supervisor Tsukada, however, insisted there must be some explanation.

"I just don't think she would leave without telling us."

"Really?" one of the older cleaning ladies said doubtfully. "You don't think it's the usual thing happening again?"

"No, I don't. She's just not the type to quit without a good reason," Supervisor Tsukada repeated.

"I don't think so either," Supervisor Hamamoto said.

"Oh, so you agree, Supervisor Hamamoto?"

"Yes. She is giving the training her all."

"It's precisely the ones who give their all who suddenly quit!" This was from another older member of staff.

Supervisor Tsukada shook her head, adamant.

"No. When you've been on the job as long as I have, you can tell immediately, from the look in their eyes. This one's a keeper. I'm right, aren't I, Supervisor Hamamoto?"

"Yes, you are."

"Hmm. I don't know about that . . . ," the other woman said.

"And anyway, she told us: 'This job is really fun!' Didn't she? Supervisor Hamamoto? Supervisor Tachibana?"

"Yes, she did," Supervisor Hamamoto said.

"She did," Supervisor Tachibana confirmed.

"A group of us went drinking a couple days ago, you see," Supervisor Tsukada explained. "Well, why not, we thought, seeing as only about a third of the rooms were occupied. Work was over by three. The four of us left work and went straight to that cheap *kushikatsu* bar by the station, for drinks and skewered meats."

"The four of you?"

"Yes. Supervisors Nakata, Nonomura, and Hori were all off that day."

"But what about Supervisor Gondo?" asked one

of the older staff, her voice very soft, perhaps hoping I wouldn't hear. "Didn't she go?"

"Oh, come on. You know she's a teetotaler!" Supervisor Tsukada replied. "It's not fair to include people like that! It only makes them feel bad."

"Yes, and anyway, Supervisor Gondo was off that day, too," Supervisor Tachibana added.

"Was she? That's odd. I thought I saw her."

"Really? You're imagining things, I think, Supervisor Hamamoto. Supervisor Shinjo was grumbling about having to do an inventory of all the supplies since Supervisor Gondo wasn't around."

"Oh, okay."

"So anyway, it was in the bar that she told us. Straight up. 'This job is really fun!' she said. 'I want to work here as long as I can!' She stuck her chest out, like this, and announced it," said Supervisor Tsukada, imitating the Woman in the Purple Skirt.

"Really? Sounds to me like she was drunk!"

"Well, she was drunk, that's true."

"Maybe she has a hangover today, and can't get out of bed?"

"Come on, that was two days ago. A hangover doesn't last for two whole days!"

"Who knows? She did have an awful lot to drink. Maybe it's still in her system."

"Well, I guess you ought to know, Supervisor Hamamoto. You had quite a bit to drink yourself!"

"Not as much as you, Supervisor Tachibana."

"Me? Well, I know I had a few. But nothing compared to all the plum and *shochu* grog you were chugging down!"

"Oh, come on now. I think of the two of us, I was rather moderate. I noticed you got hooked on the shots of whiskey right from the start!"

"Well, I don't know about that!"

"Oh, for heaven's sake!" Supervisor Tsukada said. "We all drank more than we should have. It was 'ladies' day,' after all."

"And you, Supervisor Tsukada—well, you were under the table!"

Wa ha ha. All three laughed uproariously. Just

then the director called from the other end of the corridor.

"Tsukada-saaan! Hino-san has just telephoned: she'll be coming in a bit late."

Supervisor Tsukada turned in his direction and gestured with her hands—"Got it!" She turned back with a triumphant look. "See? What did I tell you? She hasn't quit after all."

IN HER TELEPHONE CALL FROM THE POLICE box, the Woman in the Purple Skirt appeared to have given the director a full account of what happened.

The director was treating her to a can of hot coffee from the vending machine.

"*Otsukare-san*. That must have been quite a shock this morning."

It was three in the afternoon. The Woman in the Purple Skirt, who had come down to the cafeteria for a belated midday break, deferentially accepted the coffee he held out to her, and bowed her head.

"I'm terribly sorry to have been the cause of so much trouble."

"Not at all," the director replied. "You haven't been the cause of the trouble. You're the victim in all of this. There's nothing to apologize for. The person at fault is that pervert who groped you. What a creep.

As a man myself, I find it inexcusable. You must have been terrified."

The Woman in the Purple Skirt dipped her head.

"It might be best to come in on an earlier or a later bus. The perpetrator has been apprehended, I know, but even so: you never know if someone like that might sneak up on you again."

"Yes. But there isn't another bus that gets me here at the right time. The one that comes before arrives far too early, and the one that comes after gets me in too late."

"Hmm. That is a concern. . . ."

"But it's quite all right! If anything happens to me, I'm sure the other passengers and the driver will come to my rescue."

"Really? You say that, but . . ."

"It's quite all right. Please don't worry about me."

"No, but it is concerning. I was quite worried this morning. Although you made it here safely, there was no word from you even after the morning meeting started. You know I told you that our new employees sometimes just quit, with no notice."

"I would never do that!"

"I know you wouldn't. And the floor supervisors all insisted you wouldn't. Did I hear you went drinking with them a couple days ago?"

"Yes. I was just about to head home when they invited me to go with them."

"I hear you can really hold your alcohol. That surprised me."

"Oh no! Did somebody say something?"

"No, no, don't worry, it's good. Very promising. . . . You can handle your job, and you can also hold your alcohol."

"Oh, but actually that's not true. Quite the opposite, in fact. If anything, they didn't let me say no. At some point I began to feel like I might throw up, and well, frankly, I have no idea how I managed to get home. . . ."

"Really? Hm. That sounds dangerous."

"And also, I don't think I deserve any credit for

being good at my job. I think it's all because Supervisor Tsukada explains everything so well."

"Ha ha ha. Well, I'll make sure to tell her that. And I'll let her know you're hoping to take over for her eventually."

"Oh, but . . . that's not what I said."

"I'm only joking, don't worry. But, well, it's something you might consider. . . ."

"What?"

"Well, this is strictly between you and me, but at some point I'm thinking of relieving you of housekeeping and making you one of the in-house trainers."

"Me? One of the trainers?"

"Well, I don't mean immediately. But I intend to, as soon as I can. So when your training finishes, I want you to start preparing yourself to be a supervisor."

"Really? That may be more than I can handle. . . ."

"Nonsense. Look, it doesn't take any particular skill to be in that job. Surely that should be clear. All you have to do is look at those women—every one of them careless as can be. One or two of them are so lazy that the minute they become supervisors they begin to think they can do whatever they want, and begin blowing off work. I think you might add an element of freshness, Hino-san, if you were to join them—they definitely need someone to make them sit up a little. Still, I'm afraid this won't make any difference to your terms of employment—you won't get any perks, and your uniform will be the same one you have now. At most, you could expect your pay to go up about thirty yen per hour. Of course, if you stay, you'll eventually be considered for a promotion to a regular member of the staff, and, if you wanted to, depending on the results of an assessment you'd have to take, there might even be the possibility of getting assigned to the head office. Did I hear from Supervisor Tsukada that you made a declaration that you wanted to do this job for as long as you possibly could?"

"Em, well, I don't think I made a 'declaration' exactly. . . ."

"You know, when she told me, I felt a sense of . . . how can I put it . . . intense personal joy. That's right. Personal joy."

"Director . . ."

"That's right. I felt a kind of personal joy."

AS I EAVESDROPPED ON THIS CONVERSATION,
I found myself feeling irritated. Not once had the
Woman in the Purple Skirt mentioned that she'd
had her nose tweaked.

Perhaps she thought the person who had touched
her bottom had also pinched her nose? Well, it
wasn't him. It was me.

The next morning I took my place in line at the
bus stop, having decided on a particular course of
action. I would try tweaking her nose again. Yesterday so many people had come up to her. Hey, I heard
some pervert groped you? You poor thing, that
must've been awful! And each time someone
commiserated, she replied: "Yes, I know! It was
awful!" And: "Yes, I know! Some weirdo touched
my bottom!"

As far as I could tell, she never mentioned, not
even once, that her nose had been tweaked. I had

tweaked it—I was sure of that. Or maybe it wasn't actually her nose that I had tweaked. Had I tweaked someone else's? It was unclear. Anyway, if things continued as they were, it would be as if something I'd done had not actually happened at all.

So I would do it again. And this time, much harder. I might dig my nails into the flesh on the top of her nose, and make her bleed.

The Woman in the Purple Skirt might fly into a rage, and then grab me and drag me off the bus. But I didn't care. That would allow me to tell her who I was, and to apologize to her, and beg her forgiveness. And then we could become friends.

But despite my well-laid plans, that morning there was no sign of the Woman in the Purple Skirt.

After watching the 8:02 bus come and go, I sat down on the bench at the bus stop and continued waiting for her. The next bus would get me in late, but if that's what it took, I could accept it.

By the time the next bus arrived, there was still no sign of her. Maybe it was her day off? Impossible,

I thought, and quickly checked my diary. No, her next day off was Monday. Definitely not today.

I ended up waiting a full hour, but she didn't appear.

Since I had missed the morning meeting, I did a quick check of the whiteboard in the office for the occupancy rate and list of nonbookable rooms. In the column for "Other Items" was a catalog of the previous day's oversights, written in the director's messy scrawl—"Room 210: Tea not replenished. Room 709: Bathtub not cleaned. Room 811: Window left unlocked."—together with the usual stern warning: "NOTE: The figures for toiletries and amenities do not add up! Any items that go missing should be reported to your floor supervisor immediately!" After punching in, I took a look at the Woman in the Purple Skirt's time card, and saw that she had arrived at 8:50 a.m. This was almost the exact same time that she had arrived on her second day.

What could this mean? If she hadn't taken the bus, had she come by train? But she still would have had to board the bus to get to the train station. Had she taken a taxi? How much would that have cost—maybe three thousand yen? It was hard to imagine she had that kind of money just lying around. In which case, maybe she had walked to work? That would probably take a good two hours, and she would have worn herself out before the workday even began.

That day, however, she was even more energetic than usual.

When I peeked in on her, I saw her darting all over the room, cloth in one hand, little dust mop in the other.

"Quickly! Hurry up!" Supervisor Tsukada was saying. "Get every speck of dust!"

"Yes! Understood!" came the crisp reply.

This seemed to make Supervisor Tsukada only ratchet up the pressure.

"Five minutes left! Quick! Quick! Tomorrow you'll have to do this all on your own!"

"Got it! Understood!"

That afternoon, in the final few minutes before the Woman in the Purple Skirt was due to go home,

Supervisor Tsukada stamped her seal on a certificate, signifying that the Woman in the Purple Skirt had successfully completed the training.

This was her fifth day at work. It was unheard of for this to happen. Normally it took people a whole month, or two—and sometimes, for the slowest ones, half a year. Everyone, from the director to the other cleaning staff, was shocked.

As for what it meant for the Woman in the Purple Skirt, well, getting recognized as a full-fledged room cleaner in such a short time clearly gave a boost to her self confidence. Beginning the very next day, she would be walking around with a master key dangling from her waist, giving her access to all the rooms. As she walked past me, she seemed very pleased with herself.

This was something that everyone on staff experienced, not just her: a definite air of relaxation—call it a lightness in their step—the very second they got that official stamp certifying they've completed their training. And it's understandable. During training, their every move is scrutinized—they get told off, occasionally treated quite sadistically, made to do the same task over and over again till they get it absolutely right—so, not surprisingly, they become cowed. Their recognition as full-fledged employees means liberation—finally they can get out from under those supervisors. They can unlock the rooms, clean them, exit, and lock the doors—all by themselves. At last, they are in charge—of everything. In place of the pressure from all the responsibilities, the feeling of freedom must be exhilarating.

And sure enough, recently, some marked differences did seem to be discernible in the behavior of the Woman in the Purple Skirt, not only in the commitment with which she approached her work but also in the way she spent her days off.

For one, she was getting out much more than she used to. Of course, it still wasn't to anywhere special—just to the shopping district or the park.

And today she was back to her usual routine. First she bought some groceries in the shopping district, then a few things for her home, and once she had done that, she carried on walking till she reached the park.

"Hey! She's coming!" The children were already there.

The minute they saw her appear at the park entrance, they all ran up to her in a gaggle.

"Well? Did you bring it?"

The Woman in the Purple Skirt nodded. "Uh-huh."

"Oh, wow!" they all shouted excitedly. Pulling her by the hand, they led her over to the Exclusively Reserved Seat.

Once she had sat down, the children all crowded around. Quickly! Quickly! they urged her. From a paper carrier bag, the Woman in the Purple Skirt pulled out a box of chocolates.

She gave it to a boy. Evidently the leader.

"Yessss!" he exclaimed as she put it in his hands. Now everyone turned and gathered around him. Come on. I want one! Give me one too!

"Now, all of you, you must share," the Woman in

the Purple Skirt said in a gentle voice. "There should be one for each of you."

The children barely seemed to hear her, so eager were they to pick out a chocolate. Despite what she had said, they already seemed to be fighting over them.

These chocolates, containing the finest ganache made from specially selected cocoa beans from countries all over the world, and the purest cream made from the highest-quality milk in Hokkaido, cost 980 yen each. The lid was embossed with the hotel crest, comprising the letters M&H with a winged horse that had a ring of flowers around its neck. There was even a little card with a message from the patisserie that had made them.

Oh, yum. It's so creamy. . . . The children all savored the taste, looking blissful, as if they really could appreciate the difference between these chocolates and the cheap chocolate squares they were used to. Meanwhile the Woman in the Purple Skirt looked on, an expression in her eyes like that of the Madonna.

When the children learned that the Woman in the Purple Skirt had a job, they were all astounded. It seems they had assumed—along with everyone else, myself included—from the way she was so often seen wandering around on weekdays, that she was unemployed.

"Well, I've had jobs, but it was always on and off," the Woman in the Purple Skirt explained to the children, who looked at her wide-eyed. She seemed shyly pleased.

"What kind of work do you do?" some of the children asked.

"Cleaning work," she replied.

"You mean that kind of work exists?"

"Yes, it does!" she replied.

"You get paid just for cleaning?"

"Yes!"

"That's not fair! I clean my room every day! And the hallway. But I've never been paid a single yen!"

"Well, it's work. It's a little different from household chores," the Woman in the Purple Skirt explained. This was certainly true.

"I'm going to get a cleaning job too, then. When I grow up," one of the girls said.

"Me too!" echoed one of the boys.

"And me!" Another boy.

"Me too!" This time a girl.

One after another, their hands went up.

"Let's all get cleaning jobs in the same company!"

"Yeah!"

"You can come and work for my company," said the Woman in the Purple Skirt. "You know that big building right by the train station? The white hotel? The one with M&H in big letters on the front. That's where I work. When you grow up, you can all get jobs there."

"M&H? I've seen that."

"You can see it from the train."

"That's right. That's the one. It's visible from the train, and the bus. It's a very grand hotel. Lots of celebrities stay there," said the Woman in the Purple Skirt.

"Wow! Which ones?"

"Well, last week, Akira Mine was one of our guests."

"The *enka* singer?"

"Uh-huh. And the day before yesterday, Reina Igarashi, the starlet, stayed there."

"Reina Igarashi? How cool is that?!"

"Is she beautiful?"

"Mm . . ." The Woman in the Purple Skirt thought for moment. "Pretty average, I'd say."

"That's so cool . . . ! I wish I could meet Reina Igarashi. Do you think someone like me could do cleaning work too?" This was one of the boys.

"Sure."

"What about me?" asked a little girl.

"Of course, no problem. It's a bit overwhelming at first. But you get the hang of it."

"Isn't it hard?"

"There are some parts that can be hard, but once you've done them a few times, it becomes easy. There's nothing to worry about. If you come work in the hotel, I'll be the one who trains you."

It had been only a day or two since the director had suggested that one day he might make her a supervisor. In front of him, she had downplayed the possibility, but privately she must have been delighted. And now here she was, coming out with all these confident pronouncements. One would never have thought this newly certified housekeeper was only a few days into her job.

WHEN THEY HAD FINISHED THEIR CHOCOLATES,
one of the boys put his hand on the now empty box.

"Can I have this box?" he said.

"All right, you can have it. What do you plan to use it for?"

"To store coupons. My mother collects them to use in the school bazaars. The box she's got now is way too full!"

"I want it!" A girl spoke up.

"No, it's mine. She gave it to me!"

"I'll let you have the next one, Mika-chan," said the Woman in the Purple Skirt.

"When will that be?"

"I can't say for sure. As soon as I manage to get hold of one."

"I want one too," another boy said.

"All right. Then we'll make a waiting list. Top of the list, Mika-chan. Then it's you, Mok-kun."

"Promise?"

"Hey, I think I've seen this picture before," one girl said suddenly, peering across the lid of the box now in the boy's hands. "Now where did I see it . . . ?"

"That's the logo of the hotel where I work," said the Woman in the Purple Skirt. "The same logo is on the boxes of all the sweets I've been giving you— the cookies, the *Baumkuchen* cake, everything. It's on all the hotel's products."

"Oh. What is it? A horse?" This from the boy she had called Mok-kun.

"It's Pegasus," the Woman in the Purple Skirt replied.

"Ohh!" The girl staring down at the box suddenly looked up. "I remember! It's the same as the mark on some of our towels at home!"

"Your towels?"

"Yes. It's on our bath towels, our hand towels, and on the really small facecloths as well. They're easily the prettiest and softest of all the ones we have!"

"Hmm. Maybe someone in your family bought them at the hotel. But I wasn't aware that they were actually selling towels. . . ."

"No! We bought them at the local bazaar!"

"The bazaar?"

"Yes, the bring-and-buy sale at school! I went along with Mommy, and that's where we bought them. You mean you don't go to the bazaar, Mayu-san?"

"I have to admit, I don't."

"Really?" one boy asked with a surprised look on his face. "I always make sure to go, every time. They sell hot dogs and everything! And there's also a game center. It's a blast!"

"I see. Well . . ."

"Whenever I go, I get my mom to buy me manga and sneakers!" a girl said.

"No kidding. And when does this bazaar take place?"

"The third Sunday of every month! Next time, come, Mayu-san!"

"All right, I will. If I happen to have the day off."

Well, it appeared they were now all on first-name terms. To me, the children's faces were indistinguishable, but from this conversation I was able to divine that one of the boys was called Mok-kun, and one of the girls Mika-chan. As for the rest, there seemed to be a Yuji, someone else called Kanepon, and a girl called Minami-chan. The person they were calling "Mayu-san" was the Woman in the Purple Skirt. This conversation was soon followed by another in which "Mayu-san" entertained the children with a story of how she'd nearly brushed shoulders with a celebrity at work. The children hung on her every word.

The day after she completed her training, the Woman in the Purple Skirt was assigned to the thirtieth floor, where TV celebrities and idols often stayed. Each floor had specific cleaning teams, which meant I could hardly ever just pop by to see her. It was now extremely rare that I caught sight of her at work. In recent weeks, I was more likely to be able to get an idea of how she was doing from my sightings of her in the park and on the shopping street.

Ever since the groping incident, the Woman in the Purple Skirt had stopped riding the bus to work. I would see her take the bus home, so it seemed it was only the morning bus she avoided. The only other ways she could get to work were by train, foot, or taxi, but which of those she was using was still a mystery to me. Judging by her time card, for a while now she seemed to have been getting in a good fifteen minutes earlier than when she'd been taking the bus. In the mornings, by the time I got to the locker room, more often than not she had finished changing, and was looking at herself in the mirror and assiduously brushing her hair. With every stroke of the brush, that "fresh floral" fragrance wafted around the room. I'd given her only five days' worth of samples. Two weeks passed, then three weeks, and yet her hair was still smelling of that sweet perfume. It seemed impossible. But there was a simple explanation.

Not long before, I had seen her on the shopping street buying a shampoo refill pouch at the pharmacy, which meant she had already purchased a whole bottle of the shampoo. She must have taken a real shine to those samples I'd given her. I considered all the hotel shampoo she could have availed herself of at absolutely no charge. And not only shampoo: conditioner, body wash, bars of soap . . . I knew that nearly all the cleaning staff had bottles of shampoo with the hotel crest on their bathroom shelf at home. Everybody's hair smelled exactly the same, day after day. The only one who was any different was the Woman in the Purple Skirt, whose hair had that special floral fragrance.

A couple of days before, I'd heard Supervisor Tsukada ask her about it.

"Hino-chan. Is there a reason you don't use the hotel shampoo?"

"Em, well . . . ," the Woman in the Purple Skirt answered. She looked a bit uncomfortable.

"Well, why don't you use it? It's pretty good."

"Hm. Really?" The Woman in the Purple Skirt sounded unconvinced. She undid her ponytail.

"And after all, I mean, it's free. It's one of the amenities, so we can use as much as we want.

Everyone in the agency uses it. I think you should use it too, Hino-chan. Why not try it?"

The Woman in the Purple Skirt cast a doubtful glance at the mini-bottle that Supervisor Tsukada held out in her hands. "Em, I don't know whether I like the smell. . . ."

"The smell?"

"Yes. Don't you think there's a kind of fishy odor to it?"

"Really?!"

"Yeah. Some sort of raw fishy smell. Oh, don't get me wrong—I don't mean your hair smells of fish. Only the shampoo." And then the Woman in the Purple Skirt laughed lightly.

She may have laughed, but Supervisor Tsukada did not. I felt my heart pound in my chest. Apparently noticing how Supervisor Tsukada put the bottle of shampoo away in her locker without saying another word, and perhaps realizing she had said the wrong thing, the Woman in the Purple Skirt changed the topic. "I hope we can go drinking again soon!" she said, along with some other similarly cheery things, and for the moment, at least, all seemed smoothed over.

Now that she had completed her training, the Woman in the Purple Skirt was fast losing all trace of having once been a newbie. The moment you emerge as a regular member of the staff, the distinctions among employees with different lengths of service seem to fall away. In the cafeteria I would occasionally see her chuckling along as the older ladies gossiped away—and frankly, from a distance, I found it impossible to tell her apart from them. It was amazing how the Woman in the Purple Skirt had succeeded in making herself exactly like everyone else—in her hairstyle, her clothes, the way she carried herself, her facial expressions, and even the way the master key at her hip jangled on its chain when she shook with laughter.

But when I looked carefully, it was clear that what she felt inwardly didn't match what she projected outwardly. She wasn't actually enjoying being a part of it all—not in her heart. Even if her lips were smiling, her eyes were not. All the other cleaners had animated expressions on their faces, but she alone had a touch of sadness about her. She was forcing herself, trying to appear to be having fun so as not to dampen the mood. Hey, let me help you get out of there. It's stifling, isn't it? Twice now, I've tried to tell her this. "Hey, listen . . ." "Hello?" But both times, it was just when everyone else was talking most loudly and excitedly, and nobody even realized I had raised my voice.

How time passed. It was now coming up on two months since the Woman in the Purple Skirt had become a fully certified housekeeper. All I could conclude was that, for better or worse, she had fully mastered how one is supposed to behave at work.

It made me a little sad to think about it, but, well, what can you do? This was a job made up almost entirely of women, so it was only to be expected that the main thing anyone wanted to do was gossip. Even if you didn't enjoy it, you had no choice but to go along with it.

And there really was no end to it. On and on

it went, with one topic being discussed and then discarded for another. Today it might be about this person, tomorrow about that one. Always someone would be passing on tidbits about someone else—it didn't matter if they were a veteran member of the staff or a new employee. I had heard them talking about practically every member of the team. And not surprisingly, I now heard them talking about the Woman in the Purple Skirt.

"Hey, Hino-san's looking quite different these days, don't you think? She's not at all like she was when she first got here."

"Mm. Yes."

"She's filled out quite a bit. And she's way more cheerful, isn't she?"

"Mm. Yeah."

"When she first came, she looked so gloomy. And so pale and sickly!"

"She looks much better now. She's now definitely, shall we say, 'healthy.'"

"Mm. I agree."

So they were saying positive things about her.

And they were right. The Woman in the Purple Skirt had indeed changed quite noticeably over these two months. The change was perhaps most obvious in her face. Her once hollow cheeks had filled out, and she had a glowing complexion. In short, she had got a little plump. Although she didn't actually seem to be eating a huge amount. In the first few days, all she would have during the brief lunch break would be a cup of tea. I remember how worried I was that at any moment she might collapse.

In the café, there was a dispenser for complimentary cups of *hojicha* right next to the vending machine, and she would always avail herself of this tea whenever she wanted a drink. There she would sit, cradling the plastic cup with both hands, drinking the tea slowly, sip by sip. Even on her first day, as I recall, people would come by to chat.

"Oh, hi!" I would hear them say. "You're the new employee, aren't you? Is that all you're having—tea?"

"Yes."

"Don't tell me you're on a diet?"

"No."

"Well, that's no good, then, is it? You should fatten up a little! Listen, which one of these snacks would you like? Choose any you like. I'll pay."

Sometimes it would be a doughnut that they'd pay for, sometimes a sweet bean-jam bun, other times a roll. I had also seen her getting candy, bubble gum, *mikan* oranges, packets of cookies . . . I drank tea every day, just like she did, but nobody ever offered to buy me anything. Maybe it was because I drank my tea standing up, and she drank hers sitting down? The Woman in the Purple Skirt always drank her tea sitting all alone at a round table big enough for six people. There was something a bit sad and lonely about the way she looked. That might explain why everyone wanted to go up and help her. It was a daily occurrence for the director to buy her a can of hot coffee, but I had also seen Supervisor Tsukada give her the seaweed-wrapped rice ball that came with her udon soup lunch special. There was absolutely no need for her to bring a lunch box to work when she could fill her belly this way. And when nobody bought her anything, she could fill herself up with what was in the hotel rooms. It appeared she had now figured out how to do that.

Every once in a while, the Woman in the Purple Skirt would lock the door of the hotel room that she was cleaning. I had to assume that she had been taught this by Supervisor Tsukada and the more senior members of the staff. True, it was something everybody did, but strictly speaking it was against the rules. Normal procedure was to leave the door wide open while we were cleaning—and this applied to everyone, novice or veteran.

As for what was going on behind that locked door, well, needless to say she was dusting, wiping, washing, and vacuuming—but she was also indulging in a few other activities. Helping herself to a cup of coffee, snacking on the selection of (noncomplimentary) mixed nuts and chocolates. Maybe cramming her mouth full of what remained of the sandwiches the guests had ordered from room service. Or just relaxing on the bed, lying around and watching TV, or even falling asleep and taking a little nap. Or filling the bathtub with a little water so she could soak her feet. Maybe she was even taking a sip of champagne. Whenever she emerged from a room that had been locked, she usually had her mouth full of something.

This was the real reason she had—to use the staff's words—filled out and now looked so healthy. So it wasn't due just to my shampoo that her hair, once so stiff and dry, now had such shine and bounce. I guess this is what happens when people get all the nutrition they need—they really do start to look all glossy and new.

But then, on another occasion, I overheard talk like this.

"You know Hino-san. She's looking quite pretty these days. Do you think she might have had plastic surgery?" I assumed this was meant as a compliment.

"Come on. That's just makeup," another member of the staff spoke up.

"Hmm. So she's learned how to conceal her flaws."

"Uh-huh. She sure has."

"And she's quick about her work."

"Uh-huh. She sure is."

"'If you want a job done urgently, ask Hino-chan. It'll be done in seconds.' That's what the supervisors say."

"Yeah. Well, it's true. She is really quick."

"But you know . . . sometimes I think she might be a bit too quick. . . ."

"Mm . . . Well, there is that."

"I hate to say it . . . but . . . sometimes I think she might be cutting corners."

"Me too. I so think that!"

"I'm sure the supervisors must know that about her. . . ."

"Oh, I'm sure. But what can you do? She's their favorite."

"You know what? I've noticed there is a real difference between how she greets us and how she greets the supervisors."

"Yeah. It's her tone of voice. It's different."

"She uses one tone of voice for us and another for them."

"That's exactly it."

"And the way she leaves the carts. So messy!"

"Tell me about it. Any cart she uses, she'll leave it without some amenity that the next person has to replenish."

"A few days ago, she left me with a single bar of soap!"

"She never thinks about the person who has to use the cart after her. Just what serves her own needs."

A few hours after I'd overheard this, I went secretly to tidy up the cart that the Woman in the Purple Skirt had been using that day. This was a while after she had punched her time card and gone home. Just as they'd said, her cart had only a single hairbrush on it, and the supply of shower caps was completely gone. Maybe she had intended to replenish them early the next morning, but—I suddenly realized—she was taking that day off. Meanwhile, I should mention, I was due to come in to work as normal. Already it was two weeks since our days off had coincided. I found it very frustrating that I had to rely on staff gossip to know how she was doing, but it was still better than being out of the loop altogether.

The only thing to do was to look forward to next month's roster, when the schedules would be different.

But then another bit of gossip reached me.

This time it sprang from the mouths of the senior staff. And what I heard was so off-the-wall that I couldn't believe it. The Woman in the Purple Skirt was apparently in a relationship with our director! Excuse me—what did you say? Our director? Who had a wife and a child? It had to be a lie.

"Oh, it's true all right." Supervisor Hamamoto was taking the wrapper off a boiled sweet.

"Did anyone actually see them?" This from Supervisor Tsukada. She was opening a packet of roasted *kaki-no-tane* crackers. The aroma of soy sauce filled the linen closet.

"Somebody did. Actually, several people. Apparently the director brings Hino-chan to work in his car every morning."

"In his own car? No way! Really?!!"

The very next morning, I made it my business to investigate. And what they were saying—at least the last part—was true. The Woman in the Purple Skirt arrived to work in the director's car. This had to be why I no longer saw her at the bus stop in the mornings. The director came straight to the Woman in the Purple Skirt's apartment, picked her up, and drove her in. So that's why she wasn't coming to work on the bus.

But that didn't necessarily mean they were in a relationship. All I had witnessed was the director arrive at her apartment in his black car at 8:00 a.m. and give a little toot of his horn, and then, several seconds later, the door of Apartment 201 had opened, and the Woman in the Purple Skirt's face peered out. Smiling, she waved at the director and then, watching her step, walked gracefully down the stairs, opened the passenger door, and got in the car, after which the two of them exchanged a few words, she fastened her seat belt, and the director put the car into drive. That was all.

The question was, was there anything more than that? According to the rumors, at least, in the course of riding to work every morning in the same car, they had got more and more friendly, and finally ended up going out together. Was that really the case? I wondered.

IT WAS A SUNDAY. FINALLY IT WAS GOING TO be the two of us together. For the first time in three weeks, the Woman in the Purple Skirt and I had the same day off. Seventy degrees and sixty percent humidity—a perfect day, blue skies, not a sign of a cloud since daybreak.

At 9:00 a.m., the Woman in the Purple Skirt opened her apartment door and emerged. She was made up quite heavily, I could tell, even from a distance. Her hair was even shinier than usual: she must have brushed it last night. She came down the stairs rather slowly, and then, once out on the road, quickened her pace. She headed for the nearest bus stop, her heels tip-tapping.

No one was at the bus stop, since it was a Sunday. Today the buses would be on the Sunday schedule— two an hour between 9:00 and 10:00 a.m.

At 9:14, exactly on time, the bus arrived, and

she boarded. There was hardly anyone on it. The Woman in the Purple Skirt and I each selected our places, she choosing the third seat for individual passengers at the front of the bus, and I the long seat at the back. It had been some time since she and I were on the bus together. That in itself gave me quite a thrill. The Woman in the Purple Skirt spent the ride staring out the window, at one point taking her mirror out of her bag to study her face. Just once, I saw her get out a brand-new mobile phone (when had she bought that?), glance at the screen, and then, without pressing any buttons, put it back in her bag.

At 9:45, the bus arrived at the train station—our stop. We got off, the Woman in the Purple Skirt paying her fare, and I showing my commuter pass.

The Woman in the Purple Skirt headed into the shopping plaza next to the bus terminal. What could she want here? I wondered. But it turned out she was just passing through. From the ground floor she went down to the lower level, then up some stairs to the ground floor again, emerging right by the station.

There was a shopping strip with bars and restaurants and souvenir shops, though none of them had opened yet for the day. The only place open was a coffee shop; all the other establishments had their shutters down. The Woman in the Purple Skirt approached the coffee shop, pushed the door open, and went inside.

There were two other customers. One was a man in late middle age, wearing a gray knit cap and having a friendly chat with the owner. The other wore what appeared to be a black baseball cap and was sitting at a table deep inside the shop, his back to the door.

The one in the baseball cap was the director. As soon as he saw the Woman in the Purple Skirt, he folded the newspaper he'd been reading and moved the shoulder bag he'd left on the seat across from his.

The shoulder bag was black, the same one he brought to work. The Woman in the Purple Skirt sat down. "Milk tea, please!" she said to the owner behind the counter.

She asked the director what he'd had to eat.

Glancing at his plate, which he'd wiped clean, he said: "The morning set: coffee and toast with an omelet."

"Oh, that sounds fabulous," she said, staring at his plate.

At the exact moment the owner of the shop brought over the milk tea, the director looked at his watch. "We should get going," he said.

"Oh, wait just one second. Let me have a sip," the Woman in the Purple Skirt remonstrated. And she brought the milk tea to her lips.

When the director rose to go, he put on the sunglasses that had been on the table. They were very much like the sunglasses I often wear myself, but his looked more expensive. Well, what do you expect? I bought mine in the hundred-yen shop.

The director paid the bill at the register. Altogether the set breakfast (Set Breakfast B) and one milk tea came to 850 yen.

At 10:20 the two of them left the café and, arms linked, started walking along the shopping street. The stores were beginning to raise their shutters.

The director seemed tense: he was looking around, obviously worried about being recognized. Meanwhile, the Woman in the Purple Skirt walked along without a care in the world. The more watchful the director became, the more tightly and happily the Woman in the Purple Skirt seemed to squeeze his arm. After nearly ten minutes, they found a certain building and entered. The sign read YOKOTA CINEMA.

At 10:35, the Woman in the Purple Skirt purchased a Coca-Cola and a bucket of popcorn at the concession stand in the cinema foyer. No sooner had she done so than the director reached out, grabbed a handful of popcorn, and stuffed it into his mouth.

"Hey!" the Woman in the Purple Skirt pretended to scold him. The director laughed. As soon as they had entered the theater, the expression on his face seemed to visibly relax.

The tickets they'd purchased were for a double bill of *Speed* and *Dirty Harry*. I myself had seen only *Speed*. I seem to remember liking it, though it was a long time ago, and I could recall hardly anything about it.

The screening began at 10:45. First up was *Speed*. As I watched, it came back to me bit by bit. I had remembered the vehicle wired up with a bomb being a train, but it turned out to be a bus—although the action does switch to a train in the last part of the movie. The Woman in the Purple Skirt was transfixed, her eyes glued to the screen—she didn't touch the popcorn. The director, however, fidgeted constantly. He snacked on the popcorn, sipped at the Coca-Cola, scratched his face, nuzzled the shoulder of the Woman in the Purple Skirt with his nose, enjoying how it smelled (at least this is how it appeared to me), stretched his neck from side to side, yawned, and in the end fell asleep and snored. The Woman in the Purple Skirt gave him a glance, just once, but otherwise her attention didn't waver from the screen.

At 12:45, *Speed* came to an end. Following a fifteen-minute break, *Dirty Harry* would begin at exactly one o'clock. I was really looking forward to it. What kind of movie was it going to be?

Just then, the two of them got up from their seats. To go to the restroom, I assumed. But they didn't come back for the longest time. I went out to the lobby to see what they were doing, and just managed to catch sight of their receding figures, outside, heading toward the train station. In a panic, I hurried after them.

In distinct contrast to the morning, the streets were now packed with people. And the Woman in the Purple Skirt decided to reveal her special ability to the director.

"Watch me," she told him, and then she turned her back to him and made her way, with quick, gliding movements, just like an ice-skater, through the crowds.

The director laughed heartily. "Good! Very good!" he said, applauding from afar. The Woman in the Purple Skirt smiled brightly, looking back over her shoulder, and then waited for him to catch up. When he'd reached her, she set off again, smoothly threading herself through the crowds. Again she stopped, glanced back at him, and waited for him to catch up, smiling delightedly. The scenario was repeated again and again. Whenever the Woman in the Purple Skirt had her back to him, the director readjusted his base-ball cap repeatedly.

At 1:00 p.m., the two of them stood in front of one of the chain bookshops just by the station, browsing the books laid out in boxes for passersby. The director was paging through a monthly lifestyle magazine with "Special Issue on Ramen" in big letters on the cover; the Woman in the Purple Skirt had her head in a film magazine. But rather than reading her magazine, she kept peering over at his—she did this every time the director turned a page. I couldn't hear them, but reading her lips, I could tell she was saying, "Oh, wow, that looks so good!" It seemed they were going to have ramen for lunch.

At 1:10 they left the bookstore, and the place they headed to next was at the end of a little alley, which they entered after walking through the area of shops and restaurants near the station. It was a twenty-four-hour *izakaya*, where they serve alcohol and cheap snacks. So they weren't going to have ramen for lunch.

The director greeted the staff casually—*Domo!*—
as he pushed his way through the split curtains
in the doorway. The place was jam-packed, even
though it was a Sunday (or maybe because it was a
Sunday). I perched myself on a stool at the far end of
the counter.

"Suimasen!" the director barked. He signaled to
the staff that he wanted to order. This, this, and this,
he said. He was the one who decided what they'd
have; the Woman in the Purple Skirt sat in silence.
Amid the hubbub of all the customers, the director's
loud, easy laughter occasionally reached my ears; I
heard not a peep from the Woman in the Purple
Skirt. It seemed the director was a regular here.
About an hour after coming into the *izakaya*, he
turned to one of the chefs working at the other end
of the bar and barked, *"Suimasen!"* again. "Get me
some of that spicy stuff you know I like!" That spicy
stuff? What was that? Ah, *menma*: chili-marinated
bamboo shoots.

The director was really knocking back the drinks.
In the time that the Woman in the Purple Skirt had

had two lemon sours, he'd managed to down seven glasses of beer. At some point, an obviously inebriated person sitting next to them inquired: "Excuse me for asking, but would you mind telling me the story of the two of you?"

The director went bright red. "What do you think? Have a guess."

"Aw, okay. Well, are you her dad?"

"Correct!" the director declared.

Next, they ate a pot of kimchi gukbap. Surely they had to have eaten their fill by now, I thought. But no: to cap things off, they ordered a single toasted rice ball. This they ate together, intimately, sharing the same plate, breaking off morsels with their chopsticks.

It was 4:45. They had been eating and drinking for three and a half hours. They emerged from the tavern and onto the shopping street full of restaurants and bars, walked past the station, and headed straight for the bus terminal. The Woman in the Purple Skirt didn't seem too bad—she was quite steady on her feet—but the director appeared to be zonked. They were propping each other up as they walked, and as I followed them, I glanced behind me a few times: I hadn't actually paid for the three glasses of beer, the dish of foil-baked enoki mushrooms, or the soy sauce–marinated firefly squid I'd had at the *izakaya*, and was worried that one of the waiters would come chasing after me, but fortunately nothing like that happened.

At 5:01, the Woman in the Purple Skirt spoke briefly to the director, who was now slumped on a bench in the bus terminal. Without waiting for a reply, she headed toward the little kiosk and came back with a bottle of some sports drink. She sat down next to him, took off the cap, and handed the drink to the director. He took a swig, and then they proceeded to take swigs from the bottle in turn.

Almost immediately a bus came. The 5:05. But they didn't board it. The director was looking pale, and he was making some sort of appeal or excuse to the Woman in the Purple Skirt, waving his hand in front of his face. "If I get on now, I think I'll throw up." Almost immediately after that, the director hurried off to the men's room. The Woman in the Purple Skirt sat down on the bench, a lonely little figure, and enjoyed the last few sips of the sports drink. Then she looked down at her lap and examined her nails. She really did remind me of Mei-chan, my old friend from elementary school.

At 5:15 the director returned, looking refreshed. "Sorry! Sorry to keep you waiting!" he said, wiping his mouth with a handkerchief. Now it was the Woman in the Purple Skirt's turn to visit the restroom. Finding himself alone, the director began tapping away at his cell phone. Suddenly he looked up, as if just remembering something, and patted the top of his head. "Oh God. I don't have it," he said. He undid the buckles of his shoulder bag. "Ah, here it is." He pulled out his baseball cap and put it on. Then he started rummaging around again. "Oh God. Where are they? . . . Where are they? . . . Where are they?"

This time, though, it was a lost cause. He was looking for his fancy sunglasses. The ones he'd left in the *izakaya*, up against the wall on the table they'd been sitting at. The sunglasses I was wearing at that very moment, in fact. They were very nice—so much nicer than my cheapo ones. So sleek and lightweight—especially when you considered their size. With TOMOHIRO embossed in gold letters on the inside of the arms.

After going through his bag countless times, the director eventually gave up. He buckled his bag, and then pulled his cap down hard over his eyes.

At 5:35 a bus pulled in. The seats were all occupied by high school girls carrying tennis rackets. Shall we let this one go, too? I saw the Woman in the Purple Skirt ask the director. No, let's get on, he replied.

They boarded the bus. I also got on, letting one person, then another, then another, get on before me. The two of them stood in the narrow aisle: I also stood, though with my back turned. I had ended up right next to them. It was quite safe, though. The closer I was, the more unlikely they were to be aware of me. Behind me I heard them having a conversation. It went something like this.

Woman in the Purple Skirt: "I'm wondering what I should get my niece for her birthday."

Director: "You still haven't decided?"

Woman in the Purple Skirt: "No."

Director: "How about a stuffed animal?"

Woman in the Purple Skirt: "Yes, that might do. . . ."

Director: "She's the one-year-old, right?"

Woman in the Purple Skirt: "No, that's my nephew. My niece is six."

Director: "Oh. Oh yeah. You told me."

Was that the best they could do? On and on they went, prattling about what she should buy her niece. In the end she decided she would consult her older brother on her next visit home.

Her older brother. So she had a family.

I was pretty sure the director had a daughter, who would be going to elementary school next year, but she didn't come up in the conversation. I assumed the Woman in the Purple Skirt was aware that the director was a father? Well, I suppose I myself had only just learned that the Woman in the

Purple Skirt had a family. An older brother, and a niece, and a nephew.

At 6:05 they got off the bus. It was the usual stop—the view up the street that I always saw. Holding hands, the two of them walked along, just a few feet ahead of me. They crossed at the crosswalk, proceeded right through the arcade, and then a little ways ahead entered the bakery she knew so well. The Woman in the Purple Skirt took a tray, and on it they put two cream buns and a pack of sandwiches bound in plastic wrap. The Woman in the Purple Skirt paid. Altogether, the purchase came to 740 yen.

As of yet, not a single person had noticed her. How would they all react, I wondered—when they realized that the woman in this couple nestling so close together was actually the Woman in the Purple Skirt?

"Hey, guys! The Woman in the Purple Skirt has come home—with a man!"

As I imagined it, the first person to become aware of this would be a fellow pedestrian walking along the street. In a frenzy, he would dash into a nearby shop and, breath ragged with excitement, announce the news to the proprietor, who would then go and tell the proprietor of the shop next door, who would then go and tell the proprietor of the shop next to his. The customers would all hurriedly set aside their shopping and rush outside, and all the other pedestrians would quickly part ways to give the approaching couple room to pass. With throngs of people on either side of the street, it would be as if the couple had just got married and were walking down the aisle. *"Congratulations!"* someone in the crowd would shout, unable to hold himself back a moment longer. The children, who until that moment would have been hanging back in the shadows of the signboards lining the street, would all hop about merrily, putting their fingers in their mouths and giving wolf whistles. The shopkeepers would all press forward and shower the Woman in the Purple Skirt with presents. *"Please, dear!"* they would cry affectionately. *"A little gift from us!"* From the fishmonger, a whole carp; from the florist, a bunch of roses; from the sake shop, a massive bottle of sake. All of a sudden—perhaps it had been waiting on standby—a TV camera would zoom in for a close-up of the couple's faces. A microphone would be thrust in their direction. *"Tell us how you're feeling right now!"* And the Woman in the Purple Skirt would turn to face the camera. . . . But just then, briefly, something else would flash up in the camera's field of view. What the hell is that?

"Oh no! It's not, is it?!"

"It's the Woman in the Yellow Cardigan!"

As they emerged from the bakery, the couple once again joined hands and started walking along the road. I waited while they walked about thirty feet. But no one showed any reaction at all.

On they walked, sometimes holding hands, sometimes linking arms, first past the pharmacy, then past the dry goods store, then past the fishmonger, the butcher, the fruit-and-vegetable shop, the florist, and then past the sake store. Not a single person, whether the other pedestrians, the owners of the shops, or the shoppers, showed any reaction. Not one of them seemed to realize that the person who had just passed by was the Woman in the Purple Skirt.

The two of them walked to the very end of the shopping street, with no one paying them the least bit of attention, and then headed toward the residential district, which was now swathed in darkness. And that night, the director stayed over in her apartment.

THE FOLLOWING DAY WAS A MONDAY—THE FIRST Monday of the month. Which meant the hotel manager would attend the morning meeting.

"Ten bath towels, ten hand towels, five bath mats, ten sets of cups and saucers, five wineglasses, five champagne glasses, and three teapots." The officer was reading from a notepad he held in his hand. He had an unusually stern look on his face.

"It's not clear whether these items were taken by hotel guests, or whether they have gone missing within the hotel itself. . . ."

Here he paused for a moment and slowly scanned the room.

"And these are just the items from last month alone. I find it hard to believe that they've simply been misplaced. I can only conclude that someone has taken them home with them. Starting today, I'm going to require each floor's supervisor and the individual room maids to carry a checklist around with them, and to take inventory for every room each time it's cleaned. I hope I make myself perfectly clear."

When the housekeeping officer departed, the staff immediately erupted in protest.

"What the heck is he implying?! It's like he suspects us!"

"Overbearing twerp! What does he mean, take inventory each time? If he's so worried, why doesn't he come and inspect the rooms himself! Outrageous."

"Truly. Anyway, why would anyone want to steal ten or twenty cups and glasses at a time? To use at home? I doubt it!"

"No way! Not those things."

"The director is always bowing and scraping to that guy. That's why that guy thinks it's okay to be so condescending to us. . . ."

"The director is the older one, right? Why doesn't he just tell him to shut up!"

"Oh, he's never going to do that. Not the director. He's got other things on his mind."

". . ."

"Hey, did any of you see? Those two have both taken the day off today. . . ."

"They did yesterday too."

"Yuck! They've got nerve, haven't they!"

"Do you know how much the director's 'little lady friend' gets paid?"

"How much?"

"One thousand yen per hour. One thousand yen!"

"One thousand yen? That's more than the supervisors get!"

"Is that true?" Supervisor Tsukada, listening in silence till now, leaned forward. "Is that really how much his 'little lady friend' is getting?"

The truth was far from clear, but before you could blink an eye, everybody was telling everyone else that the Woman in the Purple Skirt was getting one thousand yen per hour. This won her yet another batch of enemies, without her even being aware of it. As soon as word got out that she and the director were in a relationship, everyone had immediately stopped referring to her as "Hino-chan." But now the entire staff, including the supervisors, started simply ignoring her.

One thing I can say about this line of work, though, is that if people ignore you, it doesn't make much difference.

As a hotel maid who had completed her training, the Woman in the Purple Skirt had no difficulty finishing any job that was assigned to her, even if nobody spoke to her the entire day. There was no need, none at all, for her to have a chat with anyone over the course of the day. The Woman in the Purple Skirt went about her work with a total lack of concern on her face.

She maintained that expression when she passed other staff in the corridors, even if they were older. One time, I got a nice little surprise: I was waiting to get in the elevator when the Woman in the Purple Skirt came rushing out of it, and we almost collided. But she was holding in her hands a trash bag, which knocked against me, causing me to lose my balance and fall flat on my bottom. The Woman in the

Purple Skirt didn't even give me a glance, and she fled the scene without saying a word.

I pretended to be picking a fuzz off the floor, then regained my composure and got into the elevator. A sweet fragrance pervaded every corner. It was the scent of the Woman in the Purple Skirt. Supervisor Tsukada described the scent as "rotten bananas." "You can always tell where the director's little lady friend has just been—from the stink of her perfume!"

I assumed the director liked her to wear it. And it wasn't only perfume that she had taken to wearing: nowadays she occasionally came to work wearing nail polish. Needless to say, this was against the rules. When Supervisor Hamamoto, who could not let this pass, told her to remove it, the Woman in the Purple Skirt simply left the room. The staff had been trying to give her the silent treatment, but it was beginning to seem like the other way around.

Incidentally, it wasn't only that one night that the director stayed over at the Woman in the Purple

Skirt's place. He visited her after that too, several times. Sometimes he stayed the night after a date. Sometimes he would just pop over in his car after work. Checking my diary, I see that the week before last, on Monday, he stayed overnight. On Tuesday he didn't go over. Neither did he go over on Wednesday. On Thursday, though, he went over, and stayed the night. On Friday, Saturday, and Sunday he didn't visit. Looking at this week, I see that on Monday he stayed over. On Tuesday and Wednesday he didn't visit. On Thursday I thought he was going to stay the night, but he stayed for just two hours and then left.

Mondays and Thursdays. Very possibly the arrangement is that on those days he at least pays a visit, even if he stays the night only sometimes.

The next day, the Woman in the Purple Skirt smells even more overpoweringly of that perfume. As she opens the door to the café, the other staff screw up their faces in disgust, hold their fingers to their nose, and, as if at a given signal, all get up to leave. With her usual look of utter indifference, the Woman in the Purple Skirt sits herself down at the six-person table they have just vacated and quietly pours herself a complimentary cup of *hojicha*.

If this was what things were like for her at work, what about where she lived? I'm afraid that things had changed here too. The Woman in the Purple Skirt had stopped coming to the park as soon as she started her relationship with the director. At first the children would look upset not to see her—"Mayu-san hasn't come today either. . . ." But after two weeks, her name stopped passing their lips. Now they had an entirely new form of amusement: unicycles. Not every child had a unicycle of their own: there were only two in total. They would amuse themselves in their usual ways, taking turns pedaling or dividing themselves into teams and having relays all around the park. As the races reached a fever pitch, occasionally the riders would come spilling out onto the sidewalk and the road. The cars would blare their horns, and passersby would make disagreeable faces, but the children would not be deterred from their games. The route took them first to the elementary school and then back to the park.

Along the way they would pass a heavily perfumed woman who stood at the pay phones in front of the convenience store. Little did they realize that she was the "Mayu-san" they used to know.

And see how their old friend "Mayu-san" now has long, pointed scarlet fingernails. With those sharp nails of hers, "Mayu-san" taps at the buttons on the pay phone's keypad. After dialing, she quickly replaces the receiver. Calls, then hangs up. Calls again, hangs up again. Calls, then hangs up. Calls, waits, then quickly hangs up. After replacing the receiver, she sighs and tuts with chagrin. On her days off, every hour she has is spent making such calls. In the early morning, late at night . . . No matter the time of day. Again and again she calls—and again, and again. Calls, then almost immediately hangs up. I have watched her do it so many times that now even I know the director's telephone number by heart.

THE WOMAN IN THE PURPLE SKIRT SEEMS TO be going through the most terrible time. She is distraught. She doesn't know what to do.

She is upset nearly every hour of the day. And what's more, she's all alone in her distress. Because what is causing it is not something you can actually confide in other people. And anyway, who is there that she could confide in? She still doesn't have a single close friend.

As far as I can tell, though, she's determined to keep denying whatever it is that she has with the director. Apparently, if anyone asks her even jokingly whether they might be having an affair, she furiously denies it.

". . . and then she said: 'No, we are *not* having a relationship!'"

"Ha ha! I can totally picture her when you say it like that."

"Does she really think people don't see through that?"

"So dishonest. . . ."

"Hey, you know how when she's cleaning a room she locks the door from the inside? Don't you think that's kind of gross? I mean, she could be doing anything in there . . . !"

"Yeah, she's probably got the director in there with her . . . ! Ha ha ha."

"Shh!"

As soon as the Woman in the Purple Skirt stepped into the elevator, everyone fell silent. The moment she stepped out, everyone resumed talking.

"Oh my God! What a stink! Like rotten bananas!"

"And did you see those nails? The color of blood!"

"Somebody told me the manager took her aside and gave her a talking-to. If she breaks any more rules, he said, apparently she'll be out on her backside."

"Well, I hope she does get tossed out on her backside—and quickly. Did you hear what she's getting paid?"

"How much?"

"Well, I heard one thousand five hundred yen per hour! Can you believe that?!"

The gossip being spread about her grew worse every day—and more and more exaggerated. And the more it swirled, the more pitiless the other staff members became.

But then, just when they had decided they could not have the director's little lady friend running roughshod over them a moment longer—if she didn't get the sack, they were going to take the matter directly to the head office—a certain rather decisive event occurred.

It was reported that some of the products for sale at one of the elementary school bazaars were suspiciously like the complimentary items offered to hotel guests.

The person who made the report did not leave a name. Immediately an official from the hotel rushed over to the school to investigate, and confirmed that the items were indeed taken from the hotel. Ten bath towels, ten hand towels, and five bath mats— exactly what had gone missing the previous month.

And who had been selling them? Some children enrolled at that very school.

Each of the children apparently gave the same explanation. "We only set up a stall because we were asked to—by someone else." A woman, they said, had promised that she would reward them with some pocket money.

"IT'S NOT THAT WE SUSPECT ANY OF YOU." IT was a Monday. The hotel manager looked strangely calm as he began to speak. This was the second meeting he had attended this month. "The cleaning staff aren't the only ones who have access to the rooms, after all. Guests enter, of course. Bellhops, room service, maintenance staff, and others enter regularly—even people who have nothing whatsoever to do with the hotel. I can only repeat what I told you all before: Please keep a close eye on the list of supplies. If you see that something has gone missing, you must report it immediately to whoever's in charge. If anyone doesn't report a complimentary item that's missing, or marks it on the checklist as being there when it's not—in other words, if anyone attempts to cover up for missing inventory—I will want to know why. Now, ladies. All I want from you is honesty. If you come forward and own up to it now, you won't be accused of anything. But if no one comes forward, then the hotel will have no option but to report this to the police as theft, and ask them to open an investigation. I repeat: If you come forward now, you will not be accused of anything. The hotel management is fully in agreement. If there are any questions, you can call me on my personal cell phone. I'm available twenty-four hours. Utterly confidential."

Although normally the cleaning staff would have expressed outrage—"What does he mean, he doesn't suspect us? It's practically stamped all over his face!"—today they just stood there, meekly accepting his instructions. It was obvious that they were just as convinced as he was that the culprit was someone in that very room. And every one of them—not only the supervisors but also the junior staff—had one particular person in mind. There was a perfectly good reason for this: the primary school that was the scene of the crime was just a stone's throw away from that person's apartment.

"I bet you it's Hino-san."

"Yeah. Me too. I'm sure of it."

"Her apartment is right by that school. It's got to be her."

"I wonder whether the director is aware that this has been going on?"

"Don't you think he's the one pulling the strings behind the scenes . . . ?"

"Why would he do that?"

"Isn't it obvious? He's in need of some extra cash."

"Well, you don't exactly make millions by selling things at a bazaar. . . ."

"It shows how desperate he is for money, I suppose."

"Well, he needs it now that he's getting a divorce. . . ."

"What?! He's getting a divorce?!"

"Well, he's got a new woman now, doesn't he!"

"He's not getting a divorce. Just recently he was telling me about a trip he took with his wife to Ishigaki Island, to celebrate their tenth anniversary. He went on and on about it. I hadn't even asked."

"Oh. Well. Pretty soon, then, you can be sure that girl's going to find herself dumped."

"She must be stealing all this stuff as a way of intimidating him."

"Ah-hah. That's possible."

"Shh. Here she is."

The Woman in the Purple Skirt had silently appeared in the foyer outside the elevator. As usual her face betrayed an utter lack of concern.

"Thief," Supervisor Tsukada said under her breath. Maybe the lack of concern had irritated her.

"Did you say something?" The Woman in the Purple Skirt turned and looked in the direction of the voice. At long last, a reaction. "I had nothing to do with it."

"Oh really now," said Supervisor Tsukada sarcastically. "Even though the elementary school is in your neighborhood?"

"So? You think that proves anything?" The Woman in the Purple Skirt glared at Supervisor Tsukada.

There was a tense silence.

"You lock the rooms from the inside, don't you, when you do your cleaning?" This was Supervisor Hamamoto. "Do you mind telling us what you get up to in there?"

"I don't see why that—"

"Just tell us what you get up to!" Supervisor Tsukada demanded.

"I drink a cup of coffee . . . ," the Woman in the Purple Skirt replied in a quiet voice.

"From the hospitality tray?"

"Yes."

"Is that all?"

"I might also sometimes eat a cake."

"You mean a cake from the minibar? That the guests have to pay for?"

"Yes. . . ."

"Did you hear? She steals cakes from the minibar!" Despicable! The very worst kind of behavior! everyone muttered in agreement.

"Hold on a minute," the Woman in the Purple

Skirt retorted. "I'm not the only one who does so. Everyone does it—I know for a fact! And anyway, you, Supervisor Tsukada . . ."

"What about me?"

"Well, you were the one who encouraged me to do it in the first place. 'If you want to have a cup of coffee, just lock the door from the inside. The front desk is always notified automatically if you watch a video. But the minibar is safe—we supervisors can always make up some excuse for cakes and snacks going missing.' Isn't that what you said? So I was only doing what you taught me."

Supervisor Tsukada gave a sigh. "Huh. Shifting the blame."

"Well? Didn't you say that? I seem to remember you saying, 'One of us even likes to help herself to the champagne!' Yes, Supervisor Tachibana, don't you remember? That water bottle I can see poking out of your bag. It's filled with champagne, isn't it?"

"What? You actually believed that?" Supervisor Hamamoto widened her eyes. "What's wrong with you, girl? That was a joke!"

Everyone burst into laughter. Supervisor Tachibana was laughing just as hard as everyone else, holding her belly. "I admit I like my drink, but I'm not that stupid!"

Just then, the Woman in the Purple Skirt reached out and snatched Supervisor Tachibana's bag.

"Hey! What do you think you're doing?!"

The Woman in the Purple Skirt pulled out the light blue water bottle, twisted off the cap, and sniffed.

"Give that back now!"

One of the older ladies wrested the bottle and the bag from the Woman in the Purple Skirt, and returned them to Supervisor Tachibana.

"Why snatch her bag like that? How rude can you get?!"

"It's *mugicha*," Supervisor Tachibana snorted, screwing the cap back on. "No champagne in it. Sorry to disappoint you."

"If that's really what you think," Supervisor Tsukada said, "why not check all our water bottles? You can start with mine!"

She pulled her water bottle out of her bag and

shoved it under the Woman in the Purple Skirt's nose.

"And mine."

"Mine too."

"Here, smell mine."

"And here's mine."

Everyone pulled their water bottle out of their bag, one after the other, twisted off the cap, and held it up to the Woman in the Purple Skirt's face.

The Woman in the Purple Skirt now found herself penned in by a ring of faces. Powerless, she glared silently at all the bottles held out in front of her.

But what was this? If I wasn't mistaken, she was wiggling her nose. She really did appear to be smelling all the water bottles, going from one to the other, checking, quite carefully, whether any had alcohol in them. At this, everyone burst out laughing all over again.

"Can you believe this? Is she insane?"

It was only nine in the morning. The day's work had not yet begun. Not one of the water bottles had a trace of alcohol in it.

Finally, the Woman in the Purple Skirt set her eyes on a water bottle just outside the circle of women. She bent forward to sniff it.

"You idiot!" Supervisor Tsukada scoffed. "She doesn't even like alcohol!"

Just then, the Woman in the Purple Skirt, who had been keeping her eyes lowered, looked up.

"Can't you tell?" Supervisor Tsukada continued. "Look at her! The face of a straitlaced prude, if I ever saw one!"

For a brief second, there we were, our eyes locked.

The Woman in the Purple Skirt was the first to avert her eyes. She threw a quick glance at my water bottle, which still had its cap screwed on. But that was as far as she was going to go.

"Are you satisfied now?" Supervisor Tsukada said. "Not one of us is doing anything we have to feel the least bit guilty about. Except, that is, for you."

"You should admit your own guilt before slinging mud at other people!"

"Exactly! Why not do it? If you own up now, the manager says you'll have nothing to answer for!"

"Or do you want us to report you? Is that it?"

"Oh now, don't give us that dirty look!"

"If you have something on your mind, just say it!"

The Woman in the Purple Skirt stood her ground, staring angrily at everyone, but then, all of a sudden, she turned and made a dash toward a side door.

"Hey! Come back! Where do you think you're going!"

"What about your work?"

But the Woman in the Purple Skirt was gone, never to return.

THAT EVENING, AFTER WORK, I HEADED OVER
to the Woman in the Purple Skirt's dilapidated
apartment.

I'd taken it for granted that she would be at
home, but no lights were on. I strained my ears listening right outside the door, but there was not a
peep.

For a while I hung around by a wall at the side of
the road, to see if anything would happen. After
thirty minutes, I thought I might check out the park,
but just as I was getting ready to go I noticed a car
making its way along the deserted street in my direction.

The black car came to a stop in front of the apartment building. I was quite familiar with this car.
Today was a Monday. I made a quick note ("Visited") in my diary.

The driver's-side door opened, and out came the

director. I got a good view of his dark shape, even more rotund than ever, slowly ascending the external stairs to the second floor.

The director stopped outside the apartment farthest from the stairs and knocked softly. Again and again he knocked, for about ten minutes. Then, suddenly, a light came on, visible in the previously dark window. The door opened, and through the crack I caught a glimpse of the Woman in the Purple Skirt's face. So she had been home after all.

After a brief exchange, the director stepped forward and attempted to go inside. The Woman in the Purple Skirt stopped him, obviously angry.

"Don't you dare come in here . . . !"

Then I heard her ask, "How was Ishigaki Island?" referring to the trip he'd taken with his wife for their tenth anniversary. Someone must have told her what the supervisors had talked about this morning. The trip was clearly news to her.

"Why do you bring that up?" the director shouted. "It's irrelevant!"

She too shouted. "It's relevant to me!"

"I didn't come to talk about that, but about another thing!" the director yelled.

"Well, what is it? What is it you need to talk to me about?!"

"The things you've been stealing." And here the director lowered his voice.

"So, even you think I did it?"

"Well, I mean, I have seen . . ." The director glanced inside her room. "You do have stuff from the hotel here. Cups . . . glasses . . ."

"These are for me to use," the Woman in the Purple Skirt retorted. "Why would I sell any of these?"

"Also, well—the elementary school where the items were being sold is only a few blocks from here."

"I'm telling you, I would never do such a thing!"

"Shush. Keep your voice down."

"Did it not occur to you that someone else may be selling those items? Why do you assume it's me? I know—it's because you don't love me anymore. That's why you went to Ishigaki Island with your wife. . . ."

"I told you, don't bring Ishigaki Island into this!" There was a smack. The director had slapped the Woman in the Purple Skirt across the face.

"Ow!" the Woman in the Purple Skirt yelled. "That really hurt! Ow!"

"Look, sorry. I shouldn't have done that. I'm sorry. Please, calm down and listen to me for a minute. The fact is, I'm under suspicion too. They know about my affair with you, and they think I'm the mastermind behind it all! That's what they're all whispering. Ridiculous, isn't it? Impossible! Why would I sell something in a bazaar? Oh God, what a mess! I'm really in for it!"

"What do you mean?"

"Well, how else could you look at it? You must know why I've come today. . . . You don't? Well, let me spell it out for you. I want you to write out a formal statement."

"A statement?"

"Yes. Saying you were the one who thought all this up. That I had nothing to do with it! To give to the hotel manager."

"Huh?" The Woman in the Purple Skirt raised her voice a notch louder. "I'm telling you, I didn't do it!"

"You're lying."

"I am telling you the truth!"

"You are not! Stop lying to me! You used to give out cookies and chocolates from the hotel to the kids from that elementary school, didn't you? What were those, if not hotel property? Well, actually, they belong to the guests. So, in effect, you were stealing things from the guests and passing them along to schoolkids. The same kids who were selling the hotel towels and dishware at the bazaar! Did you know about that? And guess what, those kids claim they were told to do it—by a woman! Don't tell me you didn't know about it—of course you did."

"I didn't! I didn't know anything!"

"You made use of your position as a member of the staff and sold things that belonged to the hotel."

"Stop! Shut up! What do you mean, 'member of the staff'? Don't you dare take that superior tone with me. What gives you the right? Don't think

I don't know what you get up to. Taking naps every day in the nonbookable guest rooms. Locking the door from the inside. Treating yourself to a nice cup of coffee after taking forty winks. And just leaving the dirty cup there when you've finished with it. . . ."

"So what? That's nothing. There's nothing terrible about that."

"Oh? Well, actually, that's not all. That time, when was it, that Reina Igarashi was a guest at the hotel? I have a sneaking suspicion that you stole some of her underwear, didn't you?"

"Eh . . . ?!"

"Aha, so you did! I wondered what you were doing when I saw you hunched over in front of the door to her room, looking so secretive, rummaging around. You were going through the laundry bag on her doorknob, and looking for what you could find, weren't you? I saw you pull out some red frilly garment, and then stuff it in your pants pocket. I bet it was her panties, wasn't it! Disgusting. Unbelievable. Despicable. Pervert! You pervert!"

"Knock it off!" he ordered.

"You're a pervert! A creep! A disgusting pervert!"

"Cut it out! I'm telling you . . . !"

"Ow! You're hurting me! Let me go! All right, you just wait: I'm going to tell everyone all about it! I'll tell your wife, I'll tell the head office, I'll tell the hotel manager . . . !"

"Enough!" The director grabbed the Woman in the Purple Skirt by the shoulders. "I'm telling you, just knock it off! If you tell them, you're not going to get away with it!!"

And then he began to shake her, backward and forward, so vigorously that I heard a cracking sound from her neck. But the Woman in the Purple Skirt was giving just as good as she got. At the first opportunity, she wriggled out of his grip, bent down slightly, and started punching him in the belly. He groaned and staggered back, and then she kneed him in the groin and slapped him across the face. Taking hold of the railing in both hands, he tried to right himself. But the balustrade on the stairs was so rusted away that it couldn't support the heavy weight of his body. With a loud snapping sound, the balusters broke off from the base rail, and the director fell headfirst to the ground.

He lay there on the brown earth, completely still.

The Woman in the Purple Skirt descended the stairs, shaking.

"Tomo, Tomo dear . . ." She crouched down beside the prone body and extended her hand.

"Tomo dear . . . Tomo dear . . . ," she called, and shook his shoulder and back.

"Tomo dear . . . Tomo dear . . . Tomo dear . . . Answer me, Tomo dear. Wake up. Answer me. Tomo dear! Tomo dear! Tomo dear! Tomo dear! Hey, Tomo dear! Answer me!"

"Shush. Stop screaming like that," I said.

The Woman in the Purple Skirt turned to look at me. Her face was white, and covered in tears and snot.

"Let me take a look." I squatted down, easing myself between them.

First I lifted his right wrist. Then I lifted his left one. I put two fingers against his neck, and brought my ear down close to his mouth. The Woman in the Purple Skirt was quiet, observing me, waiting. There was a moment of silence. Then I looked up at her and said: "Well, that's it. He's croaked."

The Woman in the Purple Skirt said something in a hushed voice. It was so faint I couldn't hear it. It might have been "I can't believe it. . . ."

"I can't believe it. I can't believe it," she was now saying a bit louder.

"It must have been the way he fell. His heart has stopped."

"Oh God . . . Oh God . . . Oh God . . . It's not true. Tell me it's not true. It's not true. It's not true."

I shook my head. "I'm very sorry. I can't do that."

"Oh God . . . Oh God! Please! Open your eyes, darling! Wake up, Tomo dear!"

The Woman in the Purple Skirt began shaking the director's body again, desperately. I grabbed her by the wrists. "It's no use. Don't you see? He's dead. He's not coming back to life.

"Get ahold of yourself. Face the facts. He's dead.

You shouldn't be trying to bring him back. You should be trying to get away from here, immediately. Run away."

"Run away . . . ?"

"Yes." I nodded. "There's no time to lose. The police are going to arrive any minute now."

"The police?"

"Somebody called them and reported you. When they heard you screaming. You've got to get away. Before the police arrive."

"Wh-what . . ."

"Get up. Quickly."

"Bu-but . . ."

"No buts. Listen. You've got to make a run for it. Head straight for the bus stop. There's a bus bound for Komori bus terminus due at 8:02. Get on it. You've got four minutes to get there, but you have to hurry—you should be able to make it, with your background as a runner. The bus should arrive at the train station at 8:34. Get off and board a train. Look for the limited express train bound for Yamasaka. 'Yamasaka,' like the 'yama' of Yamaguchi and the 'saka' of Osaka—have you got that? In one of the coin lockers at the west exit, you'll find a black carryall. Take it with you—don't forget. In it you'll find a purse, a towel, and underwear to last two or three days. Inside the purse, in a little pocket, you'll find a five-thousand-yen note folded up very small. Would you mind using that to buy your train ticket? You'll also see some other stuff in the locker, a Boston bag, a canvas traveling bag, a big rucksack, several shopping bags from supermarkets, and various other things, but just leave those. I'll be coming right after you, so I can collect them."

"Em . . . But . . ."

"I'd really like to travel with you, but I'm afraid I can't. I'm just too slow a runner—I'd never be able to make it to catch the 8:02. But don't worry. I'll be coming on the 8:22 bus. And I'll be getting either the train immediately after yours or the one after that. You'll be all right. I'll be following you—I'll be there almost immediately. I think it's better if we go separately—this way no one will notice us. Oh yes, and if you get hungry, there's some loose change in the purse as well, so feel free to use that to buy your-self a bento in the station. Now, is there anything else . . . Oh, I didn't tell you the name of the station you should get off at, did I? It's a limited express, so it'll be only three stops. Get off at the third stop, at Santokuji Station. Third stop, Santokuji Station. Easy to remember. When you come out of the sta-tion, you should see a business hotel, the Takagi Hotel, right in front of you. It's not great, really, for a business hotel, since you have to share a bathroom. Do you mind staying there for the night? Check in, and then just go up to the room and relax. Oh, I nearly forgot. Silly me. I was about to leave you with-out giving you this. Here, here you are. This is the key for the coin locker. Make sure you lock it prop-erly, won't you? Now I wonder where you should leave the key for me? I know, how about near a pay phone? Right next to the rows of coin lockers, you'll see a single green pay phone. On the shelf under-neath it, there's a directory. Hide the key in there, somewhere in the middle."

"But . . . I'd just . . ."

"I know you might feel anxious staying the night in a place that's unfamiliar, but you should try to get a good night's sleep and recuperate. Tomorrow we'll have to start job hunting immediately. We'll try everything there is, together, systematically, looking for anywhere that will employ us, and that will let us live together on the premises. Oh, now don't make that face. Even if we don't find anything right away, don't worry, we'll be all right. I've put everything we could possibly need in that Boston bag. Provisions, changes of clothes, money—all you could need. Not in huge quantities, obviously . . . but enough to last us for a good long while."

"Well, I didn't actually . . . Um, what I was really wondering was . . ."

"Mm?"

"Why, Supervisor Gondo, are you being so . . . ?"

I suddenly realized the Woman in the Purple Skirt had stopped crying. I found myself being observed by two small round eyes. She was looking straight at me.

I shook my head a little. I'm not Supervisor

Gondo, I told her. I'm the Woman in the Yellow Cardigan.

"So, it's *you*? *You're* the Woman in the Yellow Cardigan?" I was sure I heard her say.

In fact, all she did was keep staring at me, without saying anything.

I reached out gently and tweaked her nose. It was just a few inches away from me.

"Quickly now," I said. "Time to go. Don't worry. I'll be right behind you."

"But . . ."

"Come on, there's no time to lose! Only three minutes until the bus arrives!"

I pointed to her watch. The Woman in the Purple Skirt glanced down at it and finally gathered herself together and stood up. She still looked downcast. "Two minutes left!" I shouted, and she suddenly looked up. No sooner had she started to make a dash for the bus stop than she came running straight back.

"What now? What's the matter? Just go!"

"But . . . I don't have any money."

"What?"

"I should get some money from my place. If I can't pay, I won't be able to get on the bus."

"Oh . . . I don't know—take this!"

"What is it?"

"Can't you see? It's my commuter pass! Now get going! You have one minute left!"

The Woman in the Purple Skirt sprinted off.

Very shortly, I heard the whine of a police siren. I decided it was time for me too to leave.

But I hadn't finished yet. And now it was going to get really hard.

SINCE I'D GIVEN HER MY COMMUTER PASS, I had to make a quick stop back at my apartment, to see if I could find something that might be of financial value.

When I got to my front door, completely out of breath, it was secured with a huge padlock. There was no option but to grab a flowerpot I found lying nearby to break a window, and get in that way.

I was relieved to see that the state of my apartment was no different from how it had been when I left. My futon and TV were near the window, with a few plastic bags scattered in the middle of the otherwise empty room. The electricity appeared to have been cut off: a pull on the cord of the fluorescent light in the middle of the ceiling produced just a little tinny sound. The previous Thursday, a "Notice to Tenant to Vacate the Premises" had been delivered from the court, and I had taken refuge in a manga café near the train station. I had grabbed as much as I could—my valuables, as many of my clothes as I could carry, my toiletries, food, even a saucepan—and stowed them in a coin locker in the station, which allowed me to store luggage for three days. Only that very morning I had removed everything from one locker and transferred it all to another one nearby.

It was an enormous amount of stuff, but it wasn't everything—I resigned myself to leaving items that were too big to fit in the locker, and I'd also left a few things that didn't look like they'd serve any practical purpose for the way I was going to live.

Surely there was something here among the stuff I'd left behind that I could exchange for some quick cash? I spent several hours groping around in the darkness, finally discovering at the very back of a closet a cookie tin etched with the word "Memories." By this time I'd long missed the last bus.

I was beginning to think I'd have done better just to walk to the station, but when I opened the tin I found a wooden key chain in the shape of a palm tree, an anime postcard, and a commemorative coin issued for an expo held some years ago.

The next morning I boarded the first bus of the day, with this commemorative coin gripped tightly in my fist.

When I tried to insert the coin into the fare box slot, it just rolled back out. I tried again and again. In a panic, I dropped the coin on the floor, at which point the driver turned to me with a suspicious stare and silently thrust out his hand, as if to say, "Let me have a look at it."

Examining the five-hundred-yen coin, etched with the lettering TSUKUBA EXPO '85, the driver said, "Hm, these are rare." Then, after rummaging around in a satchel that appeared to be for his personal belongings, he fished out a five-hundred-yen coin from a wallet and exchanged it for my commemorative coin. I had fully expected him to get angry and ask me what I thought I was doing using such a coin. That was a relief. I paid the fare, two hundred yen, and got three hundred yen as change.

Upon arriving at the station, I headed for the pay

phone. The shelf below the phone had two directories stacked in it. I was about to reach for the top one, to thumb through the pages, when I became aware that there was no need to. A glance to my right showed that the key had been left inserted in the door of the locker that held my stuff.

I opened the locker door and saw that it was empty. The Woman in the Purple Skirt appeared to have collected her luggage.

But she had taken everything else too—not only the black carryall I had told her to take but also the Boston bag and the large rucksack, which I had expressly instructed her to leave.

Maybe I'd been talking too fast and she hadn't understood. She must have boarded the semi-express train carrying a huge amount of luggage.

I stood by the ticket machines, scanning for women who looked like they might be softhearted, and accosting them. "Can you spare a hundred yen?" I asked three women, and, amazingly, all three placed a hundred-yen coin in the palm of my hand without hesitation.

On my fourth attempt, I clearly made an unwise choice. The woman, who at first sight had seemed nice, replied menacingly, "Get lost, or I'll call one of the station attendants!" I scurried off. I was hoping I'd be able to collect the entire train fare, forty-two hundred yen, but—I had to resign myself—I had to make do with what I had. I purchased the cheapest-possible ticket at the ticket machine, and managed to board the slow train due to depart at 7:20 in the morning.

It took me nearly six hours—six hours!—to reach Santokuji Station. Because of a series of mishaps, including a sick passenger and signal trouble, I was forced to change trains five times, but luckily was not asked once to show my ticket. When I finally arrived at Santokuji Station, at 1:25 p.m., I found myself standing on a platform that was totally un-staffed. After placing my ticket in a little wooden box positioned by the ticket barrier, I headed for the Takagi Hotel, where we had arranged to meet.

The person working the reception desk appeared to be enjoying a siesta.

I rang the bell at least five times, and was about to ring it again when out he came, yawning, from behind the partition. To my inquiries, he replied: "Nope, haven't seen anyone who fits that description."

"But you must have . . . ," I replied. "She would have checked in a few minutes before eleven o'clock last night." If everything had gone according to plan, and she'd got on the bus that departed at 8:02 and managed to board the limited express, the Woman in the Purple Skirt should have reached Santokuji Station at 10:50. Unless the hotel had been full, she definitely would have been staying here.

Making a show of what a nuisance it was to be doing so, the man flicked through a notebook with the words "Guest List" on the cover.

"Last night we had one, two, three, five guests. All men. That's all. Not one woman."

"No women?"

"That's right."

"You're sure?"

"Yes."

"Where do you think she can be?" I asked him.

"No idea," he replied.

I was now in a panic. Could she have got off at the wrong station? Remembering my assurance that I would be arriving soon—on the very next train—I considered that maybe she had waited for me on the platform, and then, when I didn't appear, she got offended, and was now keeping herself out of sight. . . . Is that what had happened?

I searched for her everywhere—all around the station, and up and down the streets. I wasn't so stupid as to go into the police box to ask whether they had seen her, but I inquired in all the shops on the shopping street, and approached various passersby.

"I'm looking for a woman, have you seen her? She's about thirty years old, with long hair . . ."

What is she wearing? people asked. I was about to tell them she was wearing a purple skirt—then clamped my mouth shut.

What had the Woman in the Purple Skirt been

wearing last night? For the life of me, I couldn't remember.

Where on earth could the Woman in the Purple Skirt have gone?

I'm still looking for her, even now.

THE OTHER DAY, ANOTHER NEW RECRUIT JOINED the company. This one seems to have had some previous experience cleaning hotel rooms. She's getting the hang of things pretty quickly, but as usual the older ladies were all grumbling that she didn't call out her greetings loudly enough. Ordinarily, they would have bullied her so relentlessly that she would have given notice within a month. If only someone were around who could give her voice lessons. Unfortunately, however, the director was in the hospital.

Recently a small group of us went to pay him a visit. Since a great crowd suddenly turning up at the hospital would probably not be appreciated, we had drawn lots to decide which of us would go. I ended up being one of the lucky four, and Supervisor Tsukada, who hadn't been selected, somehow managed to come along anyway.

The hospital that the director had been admitted

to, specializing in rehabilitation, was a fifteen-minute walk from the hotel.

We entered his ward to find four beds, two unoccupied. In one, a scrawny old man lay sprawled on his back, staring up at a small TV hanging from the ceiling.

We waited for a few minutes, and then the director appeared, accompanied by his wife.

"Director! You're able to get out of bed!" Supervisor Tsukada rushed up to give him a hug.

"Oh! Careful!" The director's wife just managed to stop her husband from folding and crumpling to the ground.

"Oh, thank goodness!!" Supervisor Tsukada took the director's hand, and pumped it up and down vigorously. "I was so worried about you!"

"Ow! Ow! Please, that hurts! Er . . . What are you all doing here?"

"What a question! We've come to see you, of course!" Supervisor Tsukada announced, sticking her chest out proudly.

"That's very kind of you. We appreciate it, very much." The director's wife bowed her head.

"You might have called beforehand . . . ," the director said.

"We did. They must not have given you the message," Supervisor Tsukada said, and then turned to the director's wife. "He's looking so much better than I thought he would. It's such a relief."

"Yes. Thank you for your concern." The director's wife smiled graciously.

Had the talk about her ruling the roost been wrong? She didn't have a trace of makeup on her face, and she seemed meek and retiring. From the moment she entered, she'd kept her hands hovering about her husband, to see to his every need.

"Yes, you look quite well! At this rate, you could be back at work tomorrow!" Supervisor Hamamoto said.

"Don't be absurd," the director said, handing his crutch to his wife, and dropping onto the bed with a pained smile.

"When will you be able to leave the hospital?" Supervisor Tachibana inquired.

"The week after next. On Thursday," the director replied.

"Oh, that's wonderful! Such good news!"

"But I'll have to use crutches for quite a while, and report to the hospital for regular checkups. Who knows when I'll be fully recovered. . . ."

"Oh, I'm sure you'll be able to do desk work. Don't worry—no one would think of asking someone with their leg in a cast to do physical labor," said Supervisor Tsukada.

"Well, yes, but I—"

"Everyone's saying how much they miss you. With you away, the hotel manager comes to the morning meetings every day. It's unbearable—such a depressing way to start the day. Isn't that right, team?" She looked around at the others.

Everyone nodded, their faces beaming.

"Did the, um, hotel manager say anything?" the director asked.

"What do you mean?"

"About . . . you know . . ."

"You mean . . . about what happened with that woman?"

The director nodded.

"He said it's now in the hands of the police. That's all."

"The police . . ." A furrow appeared in the director's brow.

"That's what he told us, at the first meeting after the incident. It's all up to the police now, where it goes from here. All we have to do, as members of the staff, he said, is to wait, and trust that you'll make as swift a recovery as possible."

"I see."

"But isn't that good news!" Supervisor Tachibana exclaimed. "To know that you'll be able to leave the hospital so soon!" Then she added: "I really thought you were going to die when I heard you were hospitalized after falling from the second floor!"

"Supervisor Tachibana!" Supervisor Hamamoto elbowed Supervisor Tachibana. "Don't say that! It's not the time and place!"

"Ha ha ha. Just kidding!"

"Well, I actually thought I had died," said the director. "When I came to in the hospital, everything around me was white. For a second, I thought, Hang on a minute, I'm in heaven."

"Thank goodness you got away with just a concussion and a few broken bones."

"We're so sorry for all the worry and inconvenience. . . ." The director's wife again bowed her head.

"Inconvenience? Nonsense!!" Supervisor Tsukada dismissed this with a curt wave of her hand. "After all, the director is the one who's the victim in all of this!"

"That's right! He's the one who had that stalker following him around for weeks!"

"None of us had the slightest idea, you know. Well, we often used to catch sight of the two of you together, but we just thought, Wow, they really seem to enjoy each other's company—wonder if they're in a relationship? Oops! Sorry! That just slipped out. I shouldn't have said that. Not in front of your wife."

"It's all right." The director's wife shook her head. "My husband seems to have been unable to tell her clearly enough that her attentions were unwelcome."

"How could I? When she was threatening me? She told me that if I didn't go out with her, she was going to hurt you and our daughter!"

"What a despicable woman!" said Supervisor Tsukada.

"Were you all right?" Supervisor Hamamoto inquired of the director's wife apprehensively. "Did anything happen to you?"

"Well, I did notice that we started getting prank phone calls. Thank goodness she didn't go any further than that! It's not so much myself I was worried about, but when I think of what she might have done to our daughter . . ."

"Yes, it's not worth thinking about. I know it would have been different if I'd actually died, but I can honestly say: Thank goodness it was me who was pushed off a building, and not you, or Arisa. Really, I thank my lucky stars."

"Oh, you mustn't say that. . . ."

"Definitely not. Whoever heard of being grateful for being pushed off a building? And why should you take the blame for what happened? The only person who bears responsibility is that woman. And she wasn't just a stalker. She was also a thief."

"No, but there are things I should have done better. I shouldn't have gone to her apartment that evening. Not without someone else."

"You're too kind, aren't you, Director. You went over to her apartment thinking you could persuade her—that there might still be time to help her."

"Yes. I told her, If you're too afraid to come clean by yourself, I'll go with you. I'll explain everything to the hotel manager, and apologize on your behalf."

"And what did she say?"

"She just lost it, went ballistic, and . . ."

"And then pushed you from the second floor."

"What a monster!"

Everyone suddenly fell silent. The old man lying in the other bed appeared to have fallen asleep watching TV. The sounds from his headphones were now mixed with the sawing noise of his snores.

The director's wife was the first to break the silence.

"Oh! I completely forgot to bring chairs in for all of you! How thoughtless. I'll just go to the nurses' station and see if they have any."

"Oh, please don't worry. It's all right. Really. We'll be leaving soon anyway," said Supervisor Tsukada.

"We brought some flowers." Supervisor Hamamoto held out a bunch of orchids purchased on the way to the hospital.

"And I brought some *purin*." Supervisor Tachibana held out a paper bag.

"Oh, that's so kind of you. Thank you for going to all that trouble. If you're not in a hurry to leave, please, all of you, do stay a while. I'll just go make some tea."

"Oh, but really, we ought to be—"

"Please, it gets boring for my husband to have no one but me to talk to."

"Exactly," the director said. "Come on, all of you, stay a little longer."

"Well, in that case, how about if I help you. Let me get the chairs from the nurses' station."

"I will too."

"And me."

"Let me help make some tea."

"Would it be all right if I use this vase for the flowers I brought?"

"Please do. Come, the kitchenette is this way."

The supervisors all followed the director's wife out into the corridor, half running, and raising a little stir of flip-flap sounds with their hospital slippers.

The room was now silent once again. The automatic door slowly slid shut, and the director breathed a long sigh of relief.

"Director." I suddenly spoke up.

He gasped. "Oh! You scared me. How long have you been there, Gondo-san?"

"I've been here all along."

"Oh. Sorry, I didn't notice you. You startled me. Well, take a seat."

The director pointed to the one folding chair, which had been propped against the wall. I unfolded it and sat down.

"Director, I have something to ask you."

"Wh-what? What's going on? You've got a stern look on your face." The director drew back slightly.

"Director, I would like to raise a rather private matter."

The director swallowed audibly. "And what is that?"

"There is something I would like to sincerely request of you."

"Well, tell me then. What is it?"

I bowed my head to him. "Please! I beg you!"

"Wh-what's the matter? This is weird."

"I would like you to raise my pay!"

"Excuse me?" the director said.

"Please! And please allow me to take out advances on my salary! I beg you! Director!"

"Well, now, hold on a minute. It's not so easy, you know. You're putting me in an awkward position, just asking me out of the blue. This is not really the time or place, is it, for something like this. . . ."

"Please! Director!"

"I said hold on! Look at me—don't hunch down into your collar. I'm very sorry, but I don't decide financial matters by myself. I have to consult with the head office. And there's also the matter that if I raise your wages, Gondo-san, I'll have to raise the wages of all the other supervisors as well!"

"Well, can't you convince the board to agree to your request? I'm sure it's within your powers! You of all people should be able to do that!"

"What are you talking about? I can't do that. That's far too simplistic. For someone to get a raise, they first have to be reviewed by the board. And for them to even be considered, they have to be deemed extraordinarily good at their job, and enthusiastic about it. Even if you did manage to get reviewed, do you really think, Gondo-san, that someone like you would stand a chance? It's a wonder to me that you haven't been fired yet. Arriving late, leaving early, taking days off without notice. Do you have any idea how many complaints have been made about you by the other staff, saying that even when you do come to work, you often just take off somewhere and disappear? No way are you ever going to get a raise. Absolutely not."

"In that case, give me a loan."

"Come again?"

"Please! I'm completely broke!"

"Why on earth do you think I should lend you money?"

"Why not? You are my boss!"

"That's irrelevant!"

"I don't even have my commuter pass now. . . ."

"What's that got to do with me, for God's sake!"

"I have to walk to work every day. From a manga café!"

"What? What happened to your home?"

"I couldn't pay my rent. I was evicted."

"Well, I mean, that's—"

"Please! I'm begging you, Director!"

"Well, come now. That's terrible, but a loan is something else. I understand you're struggling, but there's nothing I can do about it."

"Please see if you can change your mind . . . Director!"

"I'm telling you. I can't do it! Don't you get it? It's impossible! I don't understand you. Usually, there you are, quiet as a mouse, and now, the first time you open your mouth, it's to pester me for a loan? What's the matter with you? Do you have no shame? Someone at your stage in life. Don't you think you should be a little more restrained in the requests you make of others? Ah, here's a thought: Have you tried asking your family, or relatives, for a loan? Remind me, where are you from? Where does your family live?"

"Director."

"I can't do it. I told you."

"I know you stole Reina Igarashi's panties. But I won't tell anyone."

"Wh-what?"

"I promise. I won't tell anyone, I swear."

". . ."

After quite a long silence, the director muttered, "Well, I'll think about it." His voice was very subdued.

"Thank you! I appreciate your kindness!"

Meanwhile, in the kitchenette, two women were preparing the tea tray, and an excited conversation on another topic was taking place. Really? Oh, my goodness, you must be thrilled! Congratulations! Supervisor Tsukada's happy cries reached our ears from the room down the corridor. What could the excitement be about? I wondered. When I inquired, I was told that the director was going to become a father all over again. The director's wife was expecting, and the baby was due next year.

TODAY I SPENT THE WHOLE DAY EXACTLY AS I wanted.

In the morning I hung my washing out on the line, I did a little dusting, I watched television while I had my breakfast, and then, after a brief nap, I headed out to the shopping district.

Once there, I went to the pharmacy, the sake shop, and then the bakery. On my way back to my apartment, I decided to drop by the park, and sat down on one of the three benches on the south side, the one farthest from the entrance.

This is the Woman in the Purple Skirt's Exclusively Reserved Seat.

I've got to keep a good lookout. I don't want just anyone to sit here.

Which is why I have decided I should have this seat. I am well aware of the exhortation written on the notice board: "Don't hog the bench. Share and share alike." So far, though, no one has complained. If, by some chance, some special person—perhaps even the rightful owner—were to give me a tap on the shoulder and say, "Hey, that's my seat!" then . . . I would be only too happy to concede it.

After placing my shopping bag right beside me, I take out the little paper bag with the cream bun. I can feel a glimmer of warmth coming from the bread. Gently, I tear the bun in two, and lay one half on my lap. Just as I am about to take a bite from the other half, I feel—what perfect timing—a light tap on my shoulder.

I look up to see a child cackling with laughter and running away.